RIGHTS TO LAND

A guide to tenure upgrading and restitution in South Africa

William Beinart, Peter Delius
and Michelle Hay

First published by Fanele, an imprint of
Jacana Media (Pty) Ltd in 2017

10 Orange Street
Sunnyside
Auckland Park 2092
South Africa
+2711 628 3200
www.jacana.co.za

© Good Governance Africa, 2017

All rights reserved.

ISBN 978-1-928232-48-3

Editing by Russel Martin
Proofreading by Lara Jacob
Cover design and layout by Shawn Paikin
Set in Stempel Garamond 11/15pt
Printed and bound by Shumani Mills Communications, Parow, Cape Town
Job no. 003132

See a complete list of Jacana titles at www.jacana.co.za

RIGHTS TO LAND

Contents

Acknowledgements vii
About the authors ix
Foreword xi

Introduction 1

TENURE

1. A brief history of off-register tenure 14
2. Diverse forms of off-register tenure that currently survive 19
3. Attempts to enhance security and upgrade rights 26
4. Upgrading of rights and ULTRA 33
5. Arguments for and against titling 43
6. Tenure and land administration: A hybrid route forward? A Land Records Act or more flexible titling? 52
7. Registration and spatial reorganisation 63

8. The courts and the protection of family rights in customary systems 66
9. Tenure, land markets and production: A case study from Limpopo 80

RESTITUTION

10. Historical misconceptions: Chiefs and the land 97
11. Historical misconceptions: Community 100
12. Recent case studies of restitution 103
13. Implementation of land restitution 109
14. Mala Mala in Sabi Sands: An expensive illustration of some of the flaws in the system 125
15. CPAs, chiefs and ethnicity 128
16. Popular perceptions of the reality of restitution and CPAs 135
17. Recommendations for restitution 143

Some routes forward 149
Conclusions and summary of recommendations 158
Appendix: Comments on the Communal Land Tenure Bill, 2017 161
Endnotes 174
Index 185

Acknowledgements

WE HAVE DRAWN ON A NUMBER of preliminary papers by ourselves as well as Rosalie Kingwill and Khumisho Moguerane. Condensed versions of these papers are available on the GGA website. Ripfumelo Mushwana and Luvuyo Wotshela contributed to the research. We have variously benefitted hugely from many conversations with them. All three authors have drawn on their long-term engagement with research for restitution cases and the lawyers involved, especially Alan Dodson, Shirhami Shirinda and Susannah Cowen. They have also learnt from a series of workshops organised by the Land and Accountability Research Centre, University of Cape Town; the Society, Work and Development Institute, University of the Witwatersrand; Phuhlisani; and the Institute for Poverty, Land and Agarian Studies, University of the Western Cape. Thanks to all the participants and particularly Aninka Claassens, Gavin Capps, Ben Cousins, Sonwabile Mnwana, Siyabu Manona, Rick de Satge and Janine Ubink, who have been generous in including us, sharing ideas and providing us with material. Those acknowledged do not necessarily agree with our analysis on all points but they have provided inspiring ideas and also leadership in developing an impressive set of detailed recommendations to the South

African Parliament's High Level Panels in 2017. Delius and Hay were part of the team that wrote the paper on restitution and Beinart contributed to discussions on tenure. Michelle Hay would like to thank the Andrew Mellon Foundation and University of the Witwatersrand for support during some of this research. Finally, thanks to Russell Martin for his editorial work.

About the authors

William Beinart retired from the University of Oxford in 2015, where he was Director of the African Studies Centre and a fellow of St Antony's College. He has researched and written extensively on South African rural issues and environmental history. His books include: *The Rise of Conservation in South Africa* (2003); *Environment and Empire* (with Lotte Hughes, 2007); *Prickly Pear: The Social History of a Plant in South Africa* (with Luvuyo Wotshela, 2011); and *African Local Knowledge and Livestock Health* (with Karen Brown, 2013). He has worked on land reform planning and as an expert witness in land restitution cases.

Peter Delius retired as Professor and Head of the Department of History, University of the Witwatersrand, in 2016. His research has focused on the history of the Pedi kingdom and his books include: *The Land Belongs to Us* (1983), *A Lion Amongst the Cattle* (1997), *Mpumalanga: An Illustrated History* (with Michelle Hay, 2009) and *Forgotten World: The Stone Walled Settlements of the Mpumalanga Escarpment* (with Tim Maggs and Alex Schoeman, 2014). He has written extensively on rural issues and migrant labour, and in recent years has been deeply involved in research on and land restitution in Mpumalanga and Limpopo, including work for the Land Claims Court.

Michelle Hay is an independent researcher and honorary fellow at the Centre for African Studies, Edinburgh University. Her PhD, entitled 'South Africa's land reform in historical perspective: Land settlement and agriculture in Mopani district, Limpopo, 19th century to 2015' provided a long-term analysis of what went wrong with land reform policy. She has years of experience working on land reform, has published a number of articles on land history and been involved, with Peter Delius, on projects for the Limpopo and Mpumalanga Land Claims Commissions, Land Claims Court, and provided inputs to the High Level Panel on the Assessment of Key Legislation and Acceleration of Fundamental Change.

Foreword

LAND. ARGUABLY THE MOST PRECIOUS of our natural resources, it is also, at times, the most precarious and pernicious, resulting in major conflicts.

Land can be a commodity, a means of production, a political territory or a site of social identity, imbued with spiritual qualities.

Take, for example, the traditional custom in southern Africa whereby a newborn's umbilical cord is buried in the place of birth, rooting the person to their place of origin and history, which is taken to include one's ancestors, and signalling the start of a cycle to which the individual will return when earthly life ends and they return to the self-same soil. Land comes to embody the very substance and being of life itself.

But competition and contestation over land have also led to much degradation and death, not just to human beings but to the environment as well.

Recent developments, intended to place a greater emphasis on environmental concerns in global agreements, appear to be increasingly undermined by unscrupulous governance, not least of which is Donald Trump's withdrawal from the Paris Accord, despite overwhelming global protest. Bad governance is short-termist, whereas good governance requires an ethical long game.

For all these reasons Good Governance Africa (GGA) recognises land to be a key natural resource that merits much more attention.

GGA is a leading research and advocacy non-profit organisation, which seeks to build a bridge between government and the private sector in all African countries, while strengthening civil society and promoting democracy.

As such, this current volume represents the first of two books dedicated to the topic of land as part of our Natural Resources Programme, which emphasises enhanced governance, stewardship and sustainability, especially in respect of Africa's non-renewable resources.

Our interest is broad and deep; we are concerned with anything and everything, from water and wildlife to hydrocarbons and diverse mineral resources. Our continent's wealth ought not to be our curse, but our blessing.

Conceived within this context, GGA commissioned Professors William Beinart and Peter Delius of the universities of Oxford and the Witwatersrand (Wits) respectively to lead this project. Their contribution and that of Dr Michelle Hay of Edinburgh, makes a welcome addition to the debate surrounding land. Theirs is a focused engagement on the specific issues of land tenure, titling and restitution in South Africa.

Their analysis chimes with GGA's wider concern with developments in this domain both in South Africa and across the African continent.

Whereas South Africa has been recognised globally for its remarkably innovative constitution and its progressive and independent judiciary, which has developed protection of human rights and justiciable socioeconomic rights, there remain forces within the democracy that appear to be opposed to these gains. This theme is emphasised in the current book.

The authors argue against a nostalgic return to traditionalist and non-democratic sources of authority that, in the interest of political expediency, invoke a particular version of custom.

Mahmood Mamdani, in his classic work, *Citizen and Subject*, writes: 'without a democratisation of rural customary power, urban civil power must inevitably degenerate. So long as rural power is organised as a fused authority that denies rights in the name of enforcing custom, civil society will remain an urban phenomenon. Surrounded by tribally organised customary powers, urban civil society is subject to a dual pressure: deracialisation from within and retribalisation from without. We can see this reflected in the dilemma that the ANC faced in the 1994 elections.'

This dilemma appears to have been ongoing within the ANC-led government in post-1994 South Africa. The increasing polarisation between the forward-looking rights proponents and those of the retro-tribal approach under the Zuma administration, to which our authors refer, is a subject of concern. Mamdani argued in 1996 that, 'In South Africa, though home of the strongest and the most imaginative civil society based resistance on the continent, reform has floundered on the walls of customary power'. The outcomes are not yet so definitively decided, but it is clear that rural reform is crucial, failing which 'the perversion of civil society is inevitable'.

The authors argue that land ownership and administration is important to rural democracy and that this should not be placed under the control of traditionalist intermediaries. Whether in the former homelands or in urban informal settlements, control of land can underpin forms of undemocratic and authoritarian local power.

This inevitably sets up conflict with contemporary popular attempts to pursue restitution and reform along democratic, rights-based lines. The result can be an uneasy tension, especially in the absence of a consistent and rigorous approach to land ownership and administration on the part of the state.

The book is appropriately titled *Rights to Land: A guide to tenure upgrading and restitution in South Africa*. Without redress to rights, nothing will change. We believe that this offering is a practical guide to the rehabilitation of land reform in South Africa, which places strong emphasis on the issue of tenure for all landholders in the country. It may hold valuable lessons for other countries and contexts moving out of conflict or passing through a transitional phase.

As the authors recognise, there are two crucial pillars to be discussed: land tenure and land restitution. Under the first, they emphasise the lack of security of tenure and the government's failure to clarify secure rights for the millions of landholders in customary and informal settlements. They suggest that private-property rights may now be the best route forward. Unless there is something like a privatisation from below, then there may be a privatisation from above as chiefs, corporations and politically connected elites appropriate land that is under collective forms of tenure.

Against this backdrop, the upgrading of tenure with all of its associated challenges, including the progressively heated debate about private tenure, takes centre stage. While the authors argue for a clear and fundamental right to housing and residential plots for all South Africans, private tenure may facilitate the accumulation of fragmented agricultural holdings and help to unlock the productive potential of the former homelands. They consider the idea of a new land register, which records rights and expedites planning and development strategies without according private title. But this strategy has a number of problems and thus they argue for a gradual extension of a single,

FOREWORD

flexible system of titling throughout the country that works from the base of well-established institutions and professional organisations, both public and private.

The second pillar stands on restitution. This was identified as a priority of the first democratic administration with the Restitution of Land Act in 1994, which strove to give redress for the racially based dispossession that transpired from 1913 with the Native Land Act until its scrapping in 1991. While the Land Claims Commission entertained claims to the end of 1998, a 2014 amendment to the Act enabled claimants to lodge once more, until this was invalidated by the Constitutional Court in 2016. To give some idea of the magnitude involved, roughly 80,000 claims were lodged nationally by 1998 and another 160,000 by 2016.

Restitution has resulted in some important land awards to communities. But, as in the case of attempts at tenure reform, the process has become entangled with the reassertion of chiefly custodianship. This has not always worked out to the benefit of those who were supposed to benefit. The same can be said of government officials and leaders who often subverted genuine restitution for their own gain. The case of Mala Mala, where one billion rand was paid out in settlement for one game reserve, far more than the valuation of the land by the commission, suggests that the budget has sometimes been misspent. Commercially untouchable operations, such as ZZ2, also present a conundrum.

Notwithstanding the challenges, cases of genuine restitution have been noted in several cases presented by our authors. Negotiations and settlements have become more frequent. Genuine reform needs to address the problem of rent-seeking by power blocs, such as the Ingonyama Trust, and instead favour those for humble individuals concerned to put the land to use for their own livelihoods. The authors conclude by making a series of practical recommendations to remedy the status quo.

We would like the publication to speak for itself, but before letting it do so, a number of thanks are in order: first of all, to the boards of directors of Good Governance Africa (SADC) and the David and Elaine Potter Foundation (DEPF) for generously funding the project. To our authors William Beinart, Peter Delius and Michelle Hay for your rigorous engagement, strengthened by the materials delivered by the authors contributing articles to the broader research anthology, namely Rosalie Kingwill and Khumisho Moguerane, among others. To Ben Stewart, director of the DEPF, for collegial support, and to Bridget Impey and colleagues at Jacana Media for an unwavering commitment to partner with us to 'publish what we like' in order to 'improve the lives of all citizens'. Last but not least, to various members of the GGA team, Lloyd Coutts in Publications, Mandla Tyala in Programmes, and Lauren Stevens in Development, and to our wider community of office collaborators for making this project and product a reality.

We trust that you will find this guide both intellectually interesting and practically valuable in engaging with land issues to drive targeted debate and develop appropriate solutions.

Alain Tschudin, PhD
Executive Director, Good Governance Africa
August 2017

Introduction

WHEN THE DEMOCRATICALLY ELECTED government took power in 1994, led by the African National Congress (ANC), three central elements of land policy were announced: land restitution, land redistribution and tenure reform. We focus on two of these issues – the recent past and future of land tenure and the programme of land restitution.

At present the land rights of millions of South Africans who hold their land in customary tenure in the former homelands, in informal settlements and on transferred land are uncertain. The 1996 Constitution seemed to promise them an enhancement and upgrading of their tenure. This has not been effectively done.

In this book we discuss the current position and suggest how land rights may be cemented to ensure security. Tenure is important because these largely African rural communities are among the poorest and it is important that their rights are not shouldered aside. For such families, their land rights are a major asset and we argue that they should be clearly recognised. Such a strategy may also facilitate investment and production as well as rural development more generally.

Our approach is to move away from communalist and traditionalist policies and to focus on cementing individual and family land rights. All South Africans should hold their land in systems that are akin to ownership and as secure as ownership.

We also argue for an increased priority on peri-urban land and housing – the state and private sector should try to be more proactive in this respect. We suggest that there is a fundamental right to housing but not to agricultural land.

We will directly confront the question of upgrading customary land to privately held titles. For over half a century, policy-makers and academics in Africa and beyond have debated the 'tragedy of the commons' and the value of this alternative strategy. These discussions also have deep roots within South Africa itself. In the nineteenth-century Cape and Natal, the colonial authorities and missionaries established some freehold settlements for Africans. In some cases that land is still privately held with title.

In the Cape, they also introduced a halfway house called individual or quitrent tenure. Africans in parts of South Africa were able to purchase land in private tenure (though sometimes with restrictive conditions) until 1936. Though the apartheid state forcibly removed a good deal of this, some of the land they purchased remains in African hands.

Since 1991, all South Africans have been able to purchase any private land, registered at the Deeds Office, anywhere in the country. Thus private, titled tenure is not foreign to many black South Africans. The question is whether it should be extended to the former homelands and newly restituted areas, so that there is one uniform system of land tenure in the country, or whether this will create insecurity and vulnerability.

Clear and secure land tenure for all those legally entitled to it is not only stipulated in the Constitution and is essential

INTRODUCTION

for fundamental rights in the country, but may also serve as a basis for a broad-based strategy of development that will benefit poorer landholders and give them more control over the process. Since this book was completed, the government has circulated a new Communal Land Tenure Bill for public comment; we attach an appendix with a discussion of this proposed legislation.[1]

Land restitution was put into operation by the Restitution of Land Rights Act 22 of 1994, which had been carefully prepared by land lobbies and the ANC over the previous few years. Restitution was initially envisioned as a limited process to redress land dispossession that had occurred through racially discriminatory legislation and practices during the era of segregation and apartheid, from the passing of the Natives Land Act in 1913 to its abolition in 1991.

Claims had to be submitted to the Land Claims Commission by the end of 1998. This policy was only a small element in the ANC's attempts to redress racial inequalities in landholding. It was aimed at those who had suffered from particular pieces of apartheid policy, such as the Group Areas Act in the urban areas and the forced removal of African landholders in the rural areas.

However, we argue that the aims of restitution became confused with the broader aims of redistribution, which put pressure on the commission to resolve complex claims quickly. The scope of restitution has also expanded considerably to include a wider range of claims. The commission was not set up to cope with this task. Moreover, in 2014 a supplementary Restitution of Land Rights Amendment Act was passed that reopened the process for claims. In 2016, the Act was invalidated by the Constitutional Court but not before over 160,000 additional claims were lodged, some of which were even more broad-ranging than the original ones.[2] The process has become linked to the reassertion of chieftaincy.

After two decades, some of the initial restitution claims have still not been settled and we recommend strategies for researching and resolving outstanding claims. We argue against the reopening of restitution as a vehicle for land reform. However, if the government meets the criteria required to validate the Restitution Amendment Act, it is important that the state agencies, NGOs and lawyers involved are prepared to deal with the many contested claims that are likely to result.

Restitution was an important response to the injustices of the apartheid era. But it was intended as a limited and short-term process – initially to be completed in five years. It has now dragged on for more than two decades, and if the new Act comes into force, it may continue for another few decades. Restitution creates uncertainty among commercial farmers and undermines investment and production.

Communities who have moved onto restituted land have received limited support from state or other agencies to develop agricultural or income-generating activities. Restitution was not designed as a policy to expand agricultural production or other forms of rural development but as a political strategy to redress injustices of the past. We argue that land reform should now prioritise employment creation, production and economic growth in the local and national economy. It should also recognise the reality of rapid urbanisation.

Restitution should be completed and curtailed. Under President Jacob Zuma, rural policy seems to be moving towards a form of traditionalism, even tribalism. He has called on chiefs to take the lead in the new phase of restitution. He and Gugile Nkwinti, the Minister for Rural Development and Land Reform, have called for a pre-colonial land audit.

INTRODUCTION

Policy needs to move on from romantic restorationism or political tribalism. Traditional authorities have been an important pole of power in the countryside for more than sixty years, since the Bantu Authorities programme was introduced. They have presided over an economic decline in the former Bantustans. Their involvement as the major claimants in a new phase of restitution may not only ignite ethnicity and conflicting claims but facilitate elite capture of land and rural resources. Once such intermediaries control land, the likelihood is that tenure will be marked by rent-seeking rather than pro-poor policies. The best way to deal with the injustices of the past is to move forward and not backward.

We will not discuss in detail land reform as a whole. Statistics announced by Minister Nkwinti indicate that the scale and pace of the programme have increased significantly – although the government itself acknowledges that its audit is incomplete.[3] Sihlobo and Kapuya report that over 8 million hectares (ha) have been redistributed under government programmes of redistribution and restitution while compensation has been paid on an additional 2.7 million ha. And government holds an estimated 4 million ha. While we have not found figures, considerable areas of land have been privately purchased by black from white owners. If the existing area occupied by Africans in the former homelands is added, then the total of black landholdings may now be 25–30 per cent of farmland. Percentages paint only part of the picture in that land held by black people is predominantly in higher-rainfall areas.

Land redistribution remains a pressing political issue, which has been held back by chaotic land restitution. But the key question is no longer availability of land. Much of the agricultural land in the former homelands and on newly transferred farms is underutilised for farming. While there are many reasons for this, tenure insecurity is one. Security of tenure must now be addressed as a key priority in land reform.

TENURE

SECTION 25(6) OF THE CONSTITUTION entitles persons or communities 'whose tenure of land is legally insecure as a result of past racially discriminatory laws or practices' to tenure which is legally secure. Section 25(9) commanded Parliament to enact legislation to provide for such tenure security. The subsequent White Paper on Land highlighted principles in this regard and made specific reference to tenure security in the former homelands, where customary land tenure, modified by many proclamations, persists. The aim was also to unify the system of land rights and to get rid of the second-class system for black people that was a legacy of segregation and apartheid.

In one of its most glaring legislative omissions, the government has failed to address this constitutional and socio-economic imperative. Land rights for the majority of South Africa landholders who do not have private title are probably weaker and more uncertain now than they were at the time of the transition in 1994. The position is certainly more confused. Our primary aim is to advocate strategies to clarify and entrench rights.

Addressing these questions is an urgent priority for society as a whole and has wide ramifications. What is the social context of rural and peri-urban communities for whom such measures will be most important? Grants, employment and informal businesses are the vital sources of income for most of them. Housing and mobility are essential as urbanisation continues apace. Between the censuses of 2001 and 2011, the population of largely rural provinces which include former homelands – the Eastern Cape, Limpopo and North West Province – remained roughly stable while that of the Western Cape rose by 1.3 million and Gauteng by 2.5 million. This tendency continued, though less markedly, to 2016.[4] Strategies for land tenure should attempt to facilitate mobility, as well as unlock the productive potential of the former homelands.

Threats to the land of rural communities have increased in the last two decades. One key reason is mining, especially since the Mineral and Petroleum Resources Development Act 28 of 2002, which gives particularly strong rights to those with mining licences. Demand for a diverse range of minerals has changed the social geography of mining over the last half-century. It is no longer concentrated only on the goldfields of the Witwatersrand. The development of platinum, chrome and other mines has been more geographically dispersed through the northern provinces and mines have increasingly been sited on land that was formerly in the homelands. Some of this is held in customary tenure or through PTOs (Permission to Occupy), but there are also sites where the land is privately owned by tribal trusts.

In certain respects, the diversification of mining has opened opportunities for economic development and employment in these marginalised areas. But illuminating research, especially by academics at the Society, Work and Development Institute (SWOP) at the University of the Witwatersrand, has documented cases where land rights have been shouldered aside as a result of agreements between mining companies and chiefs, or where the chiefs have appropriated control of income through claims to be representative of the landholders and communities involved.

Gavin Capps and Sonwabile Mnwana have researched platinum mining near Rustenburg.[5] People in the Bakgatla chieftaincy had historically purchased land with mineral rights, but were required to register that land under the chiefs. The chiefs have been able to secure the major benefit from platinum mining through royalty revenues and, after the 2002 Act, from shares. Mining companies could in this way meet the Black Economic Empowerment (BEE) requirements and chiefs became partners in the companies. They, in turn, assumed they had powers to allocate the valuable land needed for mining to the companies.

The Rustenburg chiefs have gone further in seeking authority over the land for themselves as private owners. Although in theory the revenues are for the 'tribe', Capps and Mnwana argue that much has been appropriated by Chief Pilane and his close associates. Chiefs have now become de facto custodians and distributors of local community benefits that accrue from mining. People in the area have not only seen some of their land absorbed into mining operations, but have been denied a significant share in income from that land, which they claim was initially purchased by contributions from their forefathers. These claims have been taken to court but are, in turn, leading to divisions within the claimant communities.

In other cases, income from mines has been appropriated by elites because people had no direct control over the land or administrative structures. Platinum was found on the land of the Bapo-ba-Mogale in the 1960s and they entered into an agreement with the prospecting company, later taken over by Lonrho.[6] The area fell into the Bophuthatswana Bantustan and, when exploitation started during the homeland era, the income very largely bypassed the local community. Following the 2002 Mineral and Petroleum Act, the traditional leadership were able to secure a small minority stake as BEE partners. There had been a history of division within the royal family and the promise of new resources exacerbated it.

The Premier of the North West appointed an administrator to run Bapo-ba-Mogale affairs, but it appears that elements in the provincial government, administrators and the main royal grouping all misused the money that accrued. The issue came to court and to the office of the Public Protector, who found that of the R617 million accrued, only R495,000 remained in 2014 with little evidence of expenditures. It had apparently been siphoned off by the provincial government and remained lodged in an account bundled with other such income streams used for ANC projects and looted: R80 million of it was spent on a royal palace, offices and a council chamber for the small chieftaincy. Money was also paid to consultants and administrators. Because of the nature of landholding and administrative structures, very little of it reached the people.

In the Eastern Cape, similar conflicts have been playing out around the mineral-rich coastal strip of Xolobeni in Bizana. An Australian mining company, supported by the local chief and a BEE consortium, of which the chief was part, threatened to remove over a hundred households in order to develop titanium mining. The landholders and their supporters formed the Amadiba Crisis Committee to defend their sites and their right to be consulted about these developments. The community connected with the Legal Resources Centre in Cape Town, a group of highly effective *pro bono* lawyers, who assisted in the legal defence. Among the many issues at the heart of the dispute, which has led to local violence and the death of a committee leader, is the strength of family rights over land. There are many other potential threats to individual family landholdings, including coastal and commercial developments and new residential allocations where customary land is well situated for transport or access to conurbations.

Most of the cases we have come across where there are new threats to land result from agreements between traditional councils and external development agencies, sometimes facilitated by government. Recent evidence is provided by the public hearings of the High Level Panel in 2017, which heard a wide range of testimony on the insecurity of rights in former communal areas. In the Eastern Cape witnesses spoke of the breakdown in land administration systems, contributing to arbitrary changes in land use, often to the detriment of women's rights in land.

In Mpumalanga it was observed that 'people continue to suffer because the land is sold ... Communal land belongs to the people, it is not tribal land. It is common here in Mpumalanga where I live that traditional leaders sell land to foreigners.'

1

A brief history of off-register tenure

WE START BY LOOKING in more detail at the various land tenure arrangements presently recognised and how they are changing. Land tenure is an opaque field, fenced in by multiple old laws and proclamations.[7] There are a number of different tenure regimes in the former homelands, as well as on land that has now been transferred from white to black. We will use the overarching term 'off-register' to refer to all of the land that is not registered at the Deeds Office. While the majority of land by area is held with private title, it is likely that the majority of landholdings are off-register because the sizes of sites in the former homelands, the transferred farms, and in informal settlements are small. A recent estimate suggests that 60 per cent of landholders in the country, including both rural and urban, are off-register, most of them poorer families with smallholdings or informal urban plots.[8]

Attempts have been made to resolve the position in the former homelands, but the process has been held up because of the complexity of the issues, political disagreements and differences over interpretation of the Constitution. Key issues include: How far should legislation and the courts provide for collective or community as opposed to individual or family rights in land? Should family rights be upgraded to private title? Alternatively, should the state entrench a role for traditional leaders in respect of land? And does the state have the capacity and will to resolve and implement a clear national policy?

In order to answer these questions, and to provide what we believe to be a workable and equitable resolution in line with the Constitution, we need first to explore the recent history of tenure.

When the Communal Land Rights Act (CLARA) was passed in 2004, many academics and activists were alarmed that it gave chiefs greater authority over land and failed to improve security of tenure for ordinary or vulnerable people. It entrenched a view that people in South Africa were either citizens with full rights in a democratic country or subjects of chiefs in communal areas, bound to the laws and courts of what could be an authoritarian system which, among other things, might discriminate against women.[9] The Act was invalidated by the Constitutional Court in 2010.

We argue that it is a mistake to provide traditional authorities with either ownership of land or with strong rights in its allocation and administration. During the early decades of the twentieth century, when African communities were battling to protect their remaining land from expanding white ownership, popular chiefs often acted as a focus of resistance.[10] As noted in chapter 8, local traditional leaders can still act as protectors of popular land rights. However, the position is changing. Moreover, there is abundant evidence that in customary tenure systems, rights to land are strongest at the level of the homestead or family, with some sources suggesting that household rights to land are akin to ownership.[11] Once land had been allocated, it belonged to the family who occupied it, and could be inherited. In other words, rights to land come from membership of a family; they were not granted by a feudal landlord-chief.

We can see this in many key texts about African society in different parts of the country. Eileen Krige said of the Lovedu, in what is now Limpopo: 'There is no allocation of land except as a formality to newcomers. Land is plentiful and can be taken up at will by anyone ... A field once cleared cannot be taken from its owner even in his absence ... Freedom to take up new lands without let or hindrance today extends even to areas outside the jurisdiction of one's own chief.'[12]

In her ethnography of the Mpondo, *Reaction to Conquest* (1936), Monica Hunter, who became South Africa's preeminent anthropologist, commented: 'in the recognition of rights over certain arable areas, the Pondo approach more nearly the European conception of ownership'.[13] In this part of the present Eastern Cape, 'a woman had exclusive right to cultivate any area which she had once turned over, no matter how long it was kept lying fallow' and this right was inherited. In a recent survey of interwar ethnographies, Delius finds similar ideas reiterated in respect of residential sites and fields among the Tswana.[14]

In his book on *Customary Law in South Africa* (2004), Tom Bennett notes two different historical tendencies in thinking about African customary land tenure.[15] On the one hand, external commentators sometimes used the idea of ownership because this was so central to European concepts, even when it was inappropriate. On the other hand, colonial governments, especially those with settler populations, distinguished African systems of tenure from ownership, emphasising the limits of individual rights, because this justified the appropriation of land. The term 'communal tenure' was often used to denote such limits. Bennett criticises the use of this term if it is taken to mean that individual families had weak rights to land.

A.J. Kerr, author of the only extended analysis of customary laws of property in South Africa, considers the word ownership appropriate to describe these rights, although he agreed that it was not exactly the same concept of ownership as in European common law. It was a right that was 'good against the world'. This is an important baseline from which to understand customary rights.

Geoff Budlender, who was involved in land cases for the Legal Resources Centre, defending communities against forced removals, co-wrote an article in 1991 that took up Kerr's argument.[16] He regarded it as important to redefine African land rights accurately – not as some loose or weak notion of communal tenure but as a form of ownership. This term would both recognise and strengthen such rights in academic and political debates and in legal cases.

All of these scholars recognise that different forms of land were governed by different rights. Individual family rights were very strong over residential sites and adjacent gardens. Arable fields were also held securely by families although there were certain times of year, in the fallow season, when they could be used as communal grazing land. Individual women tended to have acknowledged rights over arable lands in their role as wives in a larger homestead. Beyond the residential sites, gardens and arable fields, the bulk of land was communal pasture and bush or forest. Here there were rights to usage as part of a local community.

The system of chieftaincy was certainly widespread and important in the history of South Africa but in some societies there were no significant centralised political authorities because of their specific histories, migrations or experience of conquest. It is often forgotten that as late as 1951 roughly 35 per cent of African people in South Africa, or nearly half the rural people, lived on privately owned farms and were not under chiefs.[17] A significant number of them lived as tenants, with elements of customary rights to land.

The 1936 Native Trust and Land Act was a critical turning point in the evolution of land rights in South Africa, especially in the former Transvaal. The Act provided the finance and administration for new or extended reserves in which Africans alone were settled. Newly purchased white-owned farms were largely settled under chiefs. Even those who may have had a degree of independence from traditional authority, as well as some of those already settled on farms, became subject to them.

Not all were forced to do so, and it became clear that ethnic organisation was the most likely route to qualifying for additional land. This process was greatly extended during the apartheid era when the Bantu Authorities Act of 1951 laid the foundation for Bantustans or homelands and a local administration controlled by chiefs.

We believe that such policies entrenched traditional authorities from above and reshaped interpretations of customary law. Whatever the historical picture, we argue that the time has come to ensure that land rights are now vested with individual families and with individuals. The implication of treating chiefs as the owners of all land once occupied by Africans leaves families vulnerable to losing their land, missing out on the benefits of land restitution, and destroying the potential for rural development.

2

Diverse forms of off-register tenure that currently survive

DURING THE TWENTIETH CENTURY, the PTO system became the most common form of government regulation in respect of African landholding in the former homelands. PTOs were a form of government regulation and control of customary land tenure. Starting in the Cape, the state gradually developed the system in different parts of South Africa. Most existing allocations were allowed and new sites, including residential plots, arable fields and rights to grazing, were formally distributed through officials and headmen. The idea was to introduce land registers and issue certificates to married men who were deemed to be the legitimate landholders. Those with such allocations had to pay hut taxes.

The PTO system was initially unevenly implemented but it was effectively extended on land purchased under the 1936 Act by the Native Trust and on land subject to betterment or rehabilitation under Proclamation 116 of 1949.[18] Residential plots were usually about 2,500 square metres (sometimes smaller in dense settlements) and arable field around 1–2 ha. The land allocations made by PTO were not formally surveyed, although they were generally roughly measured by pacing or a chain, and the boundaries were indicated and known in local oral memory. As land became scarcer in many reserved areas, PTOs were issued for residential plots only – although these too gave rights to communal pasturage.

Conditions were attached to occupation under the PTO system and the state could in theory withdraw these rights from absentees, from those who failed to pay tax and from convicted criminals. PTOs were seen by the state to allow landholding or occupation but not ownership. In theory local headmen and chiefs could be instructed to reallocate land. The system was generally adopted by the homeland governments in the 1950s and some, such as the Transkei, took on even greater legal powers over land. Yet the PTO system did give many families certificated land rights that resembled their customary entitlement – a residential plot with a garden and space for a livestock kraal, a field (except when land was insufficient), and access to communal grazing.

Over the long term, families regarded their land as essentially customary land and the PTO as a form of security. This land could not be bought or sold, although new plots could be allocated by communities acting with local political authorities, such as headmen and chiefs, and confirmed by the state.

Millions of PTOs were issued but the system was never complete. Land registers, where they were started, soon fell behind because it was difficult to maintain an up-to-date record. In most places, local Native Commissioner's and Magistrate's offices did keep copies of the PTOs issued. But as they were not surveyed, no central record was kept of the precise location and size of allocations, and there was no central record that could be searched in the manner of the

Deeds Registry. In the Transkei, the system never reached about 25–30 per cent of districts, particularly in those parts where betterment was not imposed. In these areas, land allocation and related knowledge remained largely oral.

By the end of the homeland era in the early 1990s, some PTO records became disorganised. Following the transition to democracy in the mid-1990s, PTOs were not generally or formally issued because they were seen as an inadequate and unequal right to land. They were precisely the kind of measure associated with the old apartheid era that the new Constitution promised would be transcended. But nothing was put in their place. Some provincial and especially local authorities continued to issue them when land was allocated, but their legal status was uncertain. By 2003 a report noted that 'the PTO system is fast descending into an informal system'.[19] Hundreds of thousands, probably millions, of new land allocations have been made in the former homelands since the mid-1990s with uneven certification or documentation – sometimes these are recorded at a local level and sometimes not at all.

Women often held land as widows on behalf of their husband's heirs. A significant change has taken place over the last few decades in that women can be landholders in their own right. In a 2010 survey of three villages in KwaZulu-Natal, North West and the Eastern Cape, 9 per cent of those interviewed who acquired land before 1994 said that the land was theirs and 11 per cent of those who acquired it after 1994: access to land by women who had never been married and by widowed women had 'increased noticeably'.[20] This change was echoed in interviews in Bizana, Eastern Cape, in 2011–12.[21]

Thus there are now broadly three forms of modified customary and PTO land tenure in operation: former homeland areas where PTOs were never introduced; areas formerly under the old PTO system; and the same areas where new allocations have been made either under localised informal PTO practices or without these.

In addition, the old Cape Colony introduced a form of individual, but not private, quitrent tenure under the Glen Grey Act of 1894 as well as some previous and subsequent proclamations. The significance of Glen Grey for land tenure has often been exaggerated in that this legislation was only introduced in about half of the former Ciskei districts, and seven of the 28 Transkei districts, and it was not thoroughly implemented in some of these. This system did involve survey, and records of most of the old surveyed plots are now located in the Deeds Registry offices at King William's Town and Mthatha. There is no overarching record of these grants but information collected for the National Planning Committee in the Eastern Cape in 2013 estimated that there were about 100,000 quitrent holdings in the former Transkei and Ciskei.[22]

Although the state initially planned that whole districts would be transformed into quitrent areas, new quitrent allocations were ended in the 1920s. The demand for land was such that additional allocations were made under the PTO system and its informal post-1994 successor.

In even more limited areas, African people acquired land in private, titled tenure. Expansion of such holdings was severely curtailed by the Land Acts and some of this land was incorporated into homelands where it was difficult to defend such land as fully private. Rosalie Kingwill argues that on the privately held land she investigated in the former Ciskei, 'relationships reminiscent of "customary" concepts of the family are not extinguished when title is issued. The land is viewed as family property held by unilineal descent groups symbolised by the family name. This conception diverges considerably from the formal, legal notion of land title as embodied in common law.'[23] However, legal rights in individual quitrent tenure and in areas of freehold tenure do differ from the bulk of land held in PTO and customary systems. They are surveyed, either registered or more fully recorded at the Deeds Office, and their holders have stronger formal legal rights than those who had PTOs.

Another variation on the pattern of customary and PTO tenure has emerged in KwaZulu-Natal. On the eve of the first democratic elections in 1994, the KwaZulu Legislative Assembly enacted the Ingonyama Trust Act 3 of 1994, to which all the land in the former KwaZulu homeland was transferred.[24] This was part of the bargaining that brought KwaZulu-Natal into the national settlement and first general election, including recognition of the Zulu king. The Act essentially gave traditional authorities in the former KwaZulu homeland control over the land in that area. The Ingonyama Trust in effect continued the homeland tenure system, in some areas issuing PTOs on land under the administration of local chiefs.

From 2007, however, the trust ceased to issue PTOs and opted instead to allocate land in the form of leases. Initially these seem to have been designed largely for businesses and commercial property, but in some areas this system has gradually been extended to sites for settlement. The trust has been able to increase both its control and income. By 2015 it received over R70 million in rental income from an average rental of about R1,000 – suggesting 70,000 sites had been allocated by leases. Philile Ntuli argues that the leases give a less secure right to land than customary or PTO sites.[25] The implication of a lease is that if the rental is not paid the landholder can be removed.

Land purchased by private groups prior to the Land Acts was sometimes held by trusts in which the contributors to the purchase price held an undefined share. This form of ownership was adopted in the Provision of Certain Land for Settlement Act of 1993, passed immediately before the democratic transition to facilitate purchase of land by communities outside the homelands. By this time the state was trying to move beyond apartheid restrictions and favoured a form of private property with diminishing state involvement. However, trusts were a collective form of ownership – the members did not have shares or fixed allocations that they could buy and sell as individual families.

The same principle was adopted in the Communal Property Association (CPA) Act of 1996. CPAs were planned as the main form of landholding for farms or state land transferred to communities through the new restitution and redistribution processes. CPAs generally hold land in private title but as a collective of beneficiaries who form a committee to manage and allocate the land.

CPAs did not require chiefs or tribal authorities. Thus, although they incorporated elements of customary landholding, they constituted another new system of landholding. Initially they were largely designed for managing settlements of smallholders but they also became vehicles for more intensive farming operations – for example, when restituted land included highly capitalised enterprises.

Those who are allocated formal housing in government RDP schemes become recognised title-holders, but the issuing of titles has not kept pace with allocations and there is an estimated backlog of a million.

In summary, there are different types of off-register tenure, all with a different legal status, and these distinctions shape

the way in which tenure security and control over resources are threatened:
(a) customary land without PTOs;
(b) sites with old, formally issued PTOs;
(c) sites with locally issued certificates, sometimes called PTOs;
(d) quitrent sites;
(e) outdated titles;
(f) Ingonyama Trust PTOs and leases;
(g) family holdings within trusts;
(h) family holdings within CPAs;
(i) privately owned farms where ownership is disputed between chiefs and communities.

3

Attempts to enhance security and upgrade rights

Protective or defensive measures
THIS CHAPTER EXAMINES legislative and policy measures that might produce effective security of tenure for off-register landholders, as well as enhance their rights. It is useful to separate the discussion into two sections: legislation that protects existing landholdings and tenure systems, and legislation that focuses on the upgrading of tenure. We will also deal with the question of private titling.

In the first few years after the democratic transition, and soon after the Constitution was finalised in 1996, the ANC government, through the Department of Land Affairs, passed three Acts of particular importance in protecting the land rights of those who did not have formal titles.

The Interim Protection of Informal Land Rights Act 31 of 1996 (IPILRA) attempted to give legislative force to the constitutional provision in section 25 and was aimed especially, but not exclusively, at the former homelands where the strength of customary rights and PTOs was legally uncertain. Some of the poorest people in South Africa lived in these areas and it was important that they did not become vulnerable.

In areas of the country where labour tenancy survived, notably KwaZulu-Natal and Mpumalanga, protective legislation took the shape of the Extension of Security of Tenure Act 62 of 1997 (ESTA).

In the late-apartheid period, when the pass laws broke down, and in the early years of democracy, when full freedom of movement was possible, millions of people moved to the urban areas. Many of them, an estimated seven million at one time, established themselves in informal settlements, especially in the cities. The Prevention of Illegal Eviction Act 19 of 1998 (PIE) was designed to ensure that they had some protection from forced removal.

The ANC government has in fact largely been sympathetic and cautious in trying to deal with these huge settlements, even when they are a result of land invasions or are located in unsuitable areas. The priority has been to upgrade the sites rather than remove the people. Groups in the informal settlements, working with sympathetic lawyers, have used PIE legislation successfully to protect themselves. The Act is not always popular with municipalities, which find it difficult and costly to deal with, and there have been arguments for its abolition. However, lawyers and activists working with the affected communities defend the Act vigorously. Although the peri-urban areas are a critical arena for land reform – and we will return to this issue – our focus here is largely on IPILRA.

The term 'informal' is used in IPILRA to refer to most categories of off-register landholding that we have described earlier in the book. It is not really justified to call them informal in that they include customary and PTO landholding, neither of which is informal. The intention of the framers was no doubt to be as inclusive as possible.

The wording of the Act is relatively generous to some kinds of landholders who may be threatened. Applicants only have to show beneficial occupation 'as if they were owner' for five years. This would apply to most of those who hold their land in customary tenure or through PTOs or through other 'informal' allocations since 1994. However, IPILRA excludes those who occupy land as tenants or workers, or are in any contractual arrangement. It does not cover farmworkers, for example, or those who lease residential plots or land and may therefore not cover those who have acquired land through leases from the Ingonyama Trust in KwaZulu-Natal since 2007.

IPILRA provides a form of protection against the removal of rights. The Act has been valuable in discouraging arbitrary removal of off-register landholders. However, the Act has a few serious weaknesses. It may imply that 'informal', off-register landholders have certain rights to land, but it does not state this. It only states that they have a right against removal in certain circumstances.

Moreover, IPILRA has not been backed up by administrative support. Siyabu Manona has worked on land rights in the district of Sterkspruit in the former Transkei.[26] He found that some local power-brokers, headmen and traditional councils, were removing land from poorer families or allocating land to those who could pay more. He identified cases that could have been taken to court on the basis of IPILRA. But poor families do not have the resources to do so, unless they can enlist the support of *pro bono* lawyers such as the Legal Resources Centre. In the past, district magistrates, who had multiple responsibilities, may have resolved such disputes and helped to protect landholders. But in the 1990s their administrative functions were removed.

Manona found that no officials in the Department of Justice, where magistrates were located, or the Department of Rural Development and Land Reform (DRDLR), which was responsible for land affairs, took responsibility for enforcing the Act. Local chiefs and officials were not keen to do so and had not received instructions to do so. Whatever the strength of IPILRA, it seems that there are few mechanisms of enforcement at an administrative level on behalf of those who need protection.

IPILRA also gives communities the right to deprive individuals or families of their holdings by a majority vote 'in accordance with the custom and usage of that community'. Compensation is only specified where there is disposal of the land. In other words, a family deprived of land as a result of a change in land use agreed by a community may not be protected by IPILRA or qualify for compensation. This provision was inserted in order to salvage some flexibility in land use in customary areas.

A community (and here the definition of community is critical) can decide that they want to allow mining or a plantation or a shopping area or a residential settlement on 'their' land and they can, by a majority vote, deprive specific landholders in order to facilitate this development. In the case of *Machoga vs Potgietersrus Platinum* (2006), Judge Mavundla in the High Court found in favour of a mining company that had started to mine on land which a cluster of homesteads claimed was previously part of their arable land.[27] The judge noted firstly that the chief and traditional council, who were deemed to represent the community, had agreed to the mining. It was only people from two villages among a much larger number in the former tribal authority that put forward the legal claim to the land. Secondly, it seems that the villagers had actually stopped ploughing a few years before. The judge also took into account the fact that the mining company had a valid mining licence and would lose a substantial amount of money if its work was stopped. The villagers who brought the case were not able to demonstrate that they would lose a significant sum through the deprivation.

Leaving aside the specifics of the case, three points are striking and demonstrate the potential problems of enforcing IPILRA on behalf of those who lose land. If the individual families had been owners of the arable lands, as opposed to being considered as users, then they might have stood a better chance of defending their rights. Part of the weakness of their case was that they were not able to show that they had used the arable land in the previous few years. In other words, the judge considered that their rights were in part reliant on use. The wording of the Act could potentially be interpreted in a different way, but the judge did not choose to do so.

If they had been owners, then the questions of use would not have arisen. This is a critical issue more generally in relation to customary rights to land. In chapter 8 on court cases, we argue that individual families should have secure rights beyond usage – 'as if they were owners' – both to their residential and to their arable lands.

In the *Machoga* case, the tribal authority as a whole supported the mining company and was one of the respondents. The judge found that there had been some degree of consent at this level of the larger community. In fact, the judge could have used IPILRA directly against the claimants (though he did not do so). He could have recognised that a majority of the relevant 'community' agreed to the deprivation and thus, under IPILRA, there was no defence and no right to compensation. It was a smaller 'community' of applicants (89 in all) that claimed a direct deprivation of rights in the land.

This problem of the definition of a community is a weakness in the Act and in other contexts. In the *Xolobeni* case, for example, the local chief, also a member of a BEE consortium potentially involved in coastal mining in Bizana, agreed to the enterprise and to the removal of individual families if necessary. He claimed he had the support of the traditional council in the larger area of what was formerly Amadiba Tribal Authority.

Those who opposed the mining development, organised in the Amadiba Crisis Committee, were a smaller group who were threatened directly with displacement from their land. They gained the support of the local headman, who was also called *inkosi* (chief). Because of effective legal representation, which is not based on IPILRA alone, the mining development was suspended by the Minister of Mineral Resources in 2017 and referred to a judge.

If IPILRA had been brought into the decision, the judge would have had to decide which grouping constituted a 'community'. There may be a good case, based on legal decisions concerning restitution in the Land Claims Court, for arguing that the community is the community of landholders (see below).

If the affected families had rights as families to their land, or if they had ownership, they would at least be in a position to demand compensation. It was also clear from the judgment that applicants in an IPILRA case have to be very specific about the land they have lost. It is not enough to cite an area of communal land or land on a farm. This can be difficult in respect of unsurveyed land.

Manona argues that IPILRA is unlikely to be given the muscle to operate effectively as a protection for the land rights of poor families and that policy should be directed elsewhere. That, however, may take a long time. We would argue that either an amended IPILRA or new legislation should be passed. It should be made permanent (at present it is renewed each year, pending alternative legislation on 'communal' rights). The Act should be far more specific about the strength of family or individual rights to customary land or land held through a PTO.

It should dispense with community powers to override these rights. Off-register landholders should be treated, as the Act notes, as if they are owners. And if community powers are to be included in the Act, and we would argue they should not be, then the definition of a community should be changed. The term should apply specifically to the landholders whose rights are under threat, and not to a broader political or geographic community who might benefit from that deprivation.

There is already legislation governing expropriation by the state, with compensation, which should be adequate. These suggestions would not stop development but would ensure full consultation with the landholders involved and full compensation should they or the state decide that their land rights have to be overridden.

4

Upgrading of rights and ULTRA

IN THE LAST YEARS OF APARTHEID the white government began to rethink its attitude to private tenure among African people. The apartheid system had failed to prevent mass African urbanisation and the state had at last accepted this as a reality. Moreover, the government increasingly sought the ballast of an African middle class that might defuse the most radical expressions of opposition. National Party leaders, themselves more convinced of the benefits of private enterprise, belatedly recognised that private property could be an important element in middle-class advance.

There had been strong voices from within the African population for the right to hold land in private tenure, since the time of opposition to the Natives Land Act, and especially from the 1970s. In 1978, as a response to the students' revolt of 1976, the government allowed a 99-year leasehold in the townships to some of the black urban population. After the Black Communities Development Act of 1984, this was gradually changed to freehold, once surveys had been carried out. The survey of Soweto was started in 1984 and by 1994 roughly 40 per cent of formal council housing (over 40,000 units) was privately owned and another 15,000 houses had been privately constructed.[28] This was a remarkable change with nearly half of Soweto's formal housing stock becoming privately owned within a decade. After 1991 ownership was possible outside designated townships.

At the same time, the state began to rethink its notions of occupation of land in the former homelands. Previously, land newly purchased from whites to expand the Bantustans had largely been placed under tribal authorities, but plans were developed to subdivide some of the land into small farms for individuals, rather than as customary land under chiefs. In 1991, as part of the early moves towards a political settlement, the Land Acts were abolished, enabling black people to purchase land as title-holders anywhere in the country. However, this applied only to land registered with the Deeds Office, not to the off-register landholding described earlier in the former homelands.

In 1991 the government also passed an Upgrading of Land Tenure Rights Act (ULTRA), with amendments in 1996 and 1998. It applied both to urban and rural land. In the urban areas, the emphasis was on upgrading to private title in the townships. In the rural areas, the Act potentially offered private tenure to some of the existing categories of off-register black landholders. It also provided for those holding land as a 'tribe' to upgrade their collective tenure to ownership and to compile a register of land rights in the area. Subject to a ten-year moratorium and full consultation, they could sell or let the land. The government would pay for initial survey and upgrading costs.

This seemed to be a policy direction favoured by the ANC. Newly developed RDP housing in the urban areas was also allocated with the intention that its recipients would receive titles registered at the Deeds Office. These policies would certainly have met the constitutional requirements of section 25. On the one hand, greater protection was extended to existing customary and informal landholdings through IPILRA, ESTA and PIE, and on the other hand, there was the promise of a positive upgrading towards title.

However, the direction of policy proved to be far less clear and the Upgrading Act was very partially implemented. In part this was because of a lack of clarity as to the geographical areas and types of land included under the Act. Initially the four formerly independent homelands (Transkei, Ciskei, Bophuthatswana and Venda) were excluded. When they were included in the 1998 amendment, it appears that PTOs, the most common form of landholding in these areas, were excluded from upgrading. These forms of tenure were to be dealt with under different communal or customary tenure legislation that was proposed but not passed at the time. Moreover, chiefs and traditional authorities were also opposed to the implementation of ULTRA, and in KwaZulu-Natal the Ingonyama Trust did not wish its land to be included within ULTRA's remit.

In order for land to be registered with title, the requirements of the Deeds Registry Act of 1937 need to be met, including professional survey. This was a particularly challenging task in many of the rural areas and informal urban settlements. Thus the emphasis of the Upgrading Act was initially on the urban African townships which had been formally planned in the past. It enabled those who held land in such settlements, usually on the basis of leases from municipalities, to convert their ownership to titles once their area had been formally surveyed.

RDP houses, the new houses built by the state for poor

people pouring into the cities, were similarly incorporated, and the Act was potentially applicable in informal settlements once they had been planned and surveyed and formal housing and services been provided. ULTRA provided that the state or municipality would meet the initial costs of survey and registration of the title deed.

In 2009, Umhlaba Rural Services wrote a lengthy commissioned report on the operation of ULTRA.[29] Their research, by a range of authors with different views, produced uneven conclusions. The upgrading of Mdantsane, a large township outside East London, formerly part of the Ciskei, was seen as a success: 'there is now an active and formal land and housing market as evidenced by the number of "For Sale" signs on Mdantsane properties'. Property prices in parts of the township had increased rapidly, owners were able to invest in and benefit from their properties, and more general business investment took place.

There was also upgrading in parts of Botshabelo and Thaba Nchu in the Free State, despite opposition from the tribal authorities, but in this case other planning mechanisms were used. These areas had fallen under the Bophuthatswana homeland.

ULTRA and related strategies have been most successful in existing planned townships and peri-urban contexts where there is little political resistance and the costs of implementation per unit have been low. But this process has been slow and uneven. Establishing ownership, and surveying and upgrading tens of thousands of properties, are time-consuming and evidence from the Umhlaba report suggests that it is difficult to include all properties in areas such as Thaba Nchu and Botshabelo.

With respect to RDP housing, there is a backlog in the

issuing of title deeds; some estimates suggest that this amounts to more than one million. Some informal settlements are reluctant to upgrade because of the costs of municipal rates that would be levied. Cities have battled to keep up with the growing informal settlements as people still arrive from the rural areas and rented backyard shacks.

However, urban policy and practice have been fairly consistent in envisaging that all urban property will be privately owned, and over two million 'parcels' of land have been added to the portfolio of the Deeds Offices in the last couple of decades. The sale of RDP houses was temporarily restricted, but this was difficult to enforce and most of these are now beyond the time limit. Estimates based on surveys of a few sites suggest that more than 10 per cent of RDP houses had been sold by 2007; most of these were probably sold informally and off-register.

ULTRA has not been much implemented in the rural areas, because the current schedules to the Act limit its applicability. There are difficulties involved in survey and registering communal rights (see below) and the government planned to regulate these areas through other legislation. This was passed as the Communal Land Rights Act in 2004 but it was successfully challenged in the Constitutional Court in 2010 on procedural grounds relating to the consultation process.

However, criticism of the Communal Land Rights Act focused on its failure to give effect to the constitutional protections in section 25. A key reason was that the Act privileged traditional leaders and traditional authorities in the former homelands.

ULTRA made specific reference to rural quitrent tenure in the Eastern Cape. This gave stronger individual rights to a male household head over the primary residential and arable sites.

In customary systems, all men could expect to get sites when they married. In quitrent areas, the policy was to restrict this to the heir, usually the oldest son. Land held in quitrent was surveyed and certificates similar to titles were issued to the holder but included a condition of inalienability – they could not formally be bought and sold. ULTRA clearly applied to the Ciskei properties held under quitrent and the terms of the Act seem to indicate that legal upgrading to ownership was instantaneous once it was passed.

Government officials at the Deeds Registry in King William's Town, where the quitrent records for the former Ciskei are now kept, say that in their understanding, the quitrents were all automatically upgraded when the Act was passed in 1991.[30] However, they explain further that it is not quite as simple as that: before such rights of ownership can be realised and transacted, they have to comply with the Deeds Registry Act. Many of the quitrent documents held by the Deeds Office and by families still have the name of the original grantee or a descendant from a few generations back.

For the quitrent document to be registered as a formal title at the Deeds Office, it has to be updated. The family has to register the death of the named holder, decide on a nominee or nominees to receive transfer of the property, and notify the Master of the High Court. This will usually require consultation within the family and also legal representation. An updated survey can be required too. The quitrent can then be registered as a freehold property.

All Ciskei quitrenters have the right to upgrade, but according to officials not many have done so. The government did not embark on a publicity campaign to encourage people to upgrade. The process has been left to individual quitrent holders to take the initiative; many do not know about the opportunity, and it also involves some expenses for legal services.

Upgrading also ends the conditions stipulated for the quitrent. Land with full title can be freely sold and bequeathed, subject to inheritance law. Although upgrading gives the right to sell, this does not seem to be a widespread motivation, as Deeds Office officials thought that this was rarely done. However, another change that is possible is for the land to be registered to a woman. Women did occasionally hold quitrent sites in the early twentieth century, but they were largely squeezed out in the Ciskei districts as land became short from the 1930s to the 1960s and betterment schemes were introduced.[31]

Some Ciskei councillors defended the right of women to hold and inherit quitrent land especially if they were in effect family heads and responsible for children. In 1953 the Chief Native Commissioner explicitly forbade women to inherit rights to their father's quitrent land when he died. This can now be reversed, and an example we saw of an upgraded title was in fact registered in the name of a woman. Thus in the case of quitrents at least, upgrading to full title provides potential for greater gender equality in landownership, in line with the Constitution. We will discuss the gender implications of titling later.

Conditions can still be put on a title. We examined one upgraded title, which contained a number of conditions. The most significant stipulated that the land could not be used as surety for debt other than for a mortgage on the land. This is apparently an old provision but it seems to chime with the *Jaftha* judgment (2004) in the Constitutional Court that stipulated that landowners could not be forced to sell their properties in order to cover small debts.[32] The court decided that the constitutional commitment to housing overrode the rights of creditors. There were also conditions stipulating the state's power over mineral rights on the property. We will return to this issue of placing conditions on private, titled land.

It would certainly be possible for the government to take the initiative and invest the resources in a pilot scheme to upgrade a quitrent area as a whole. However, one of the difficulties of upgrading quitrent districts is that none of them now has quitrent tenure alone.

Luvuyo Wotshela demonstrates that especially from the 1950s, as people were ejected from white-owned farms, the government provided them with PTO allocations in quitrent districts. They were accommodated with sites on grazing land. In addition, in some quitrent areas, such as Mgwali in the Border district of Stutterheim, quitrenters sublet some of their land.[33] By the 1950s and 1960s, some found it increasingly difficult to collect rents and, in effect, some of the lessees had become independent occupiers of land. The government was also keen for such African areas to absorb more of the population being pushed off the white-owned farms.

In the case of Mgwali, this history stymied attempts at a comprehensive upgrading.[34] The highly organised quitrenters claim that they have suffered from racial discrimination by being forced to accommodate former farmworkers on their land and in effect have lost substantial parts of their pastures. They insisted that they should receive restitution for their losses before they would consider upgrading. The process has proved complex and similar problems may affect many other quitrent titles. The issue arises whether both the quitrent and the newer PTO sites should be simultaneously upgraded, and who has rights to the commonage.

CPAs provide another challenge for upgrading. Much of the land that has been awarded in restitution or redistribution processes is held by CPAs or trusts. CPAs hold private titles to farms and are operated according to constitutions. Generally these provide for a committee or committees to manage the land and other economic activities.

Some CPAs are composed of a small group of families, but some include hundreds.[35] In both these cases, however, land allocations were made to families and individuals within the larger property. The rights of individual families to land do not amount to those of private owners and are subject to some degree to collective and committee decision-making processes. Some provincial offices of the Department of Rural Development have encouraged the inclusion of chiefs onto CPAs in order to facilitate their functioning and reduce local opposition.

Government has failed to provide effective oversight of the growing number of CPAs, and the land rights of individual families within CPAs are uncertain.[36] Upgrading of land rights within CPAs may be possible through a process similar to ULTRA or sectional title.

In summary, ULTRA has been implemented in some urban contexts and seems to have been successful in places, such as Mdantsane, where the demand for title is high and where land and mortgage markets are already active.

It has taken roughly ten years to upgrade townships, and it has been difficult to include all of those who could potentially be beneficiaries because of uncertainty about rights, the difficulty of maintaining long-term commitment by consultants and professionals, and the costs. These were not high, at about R600 per unit in Thaba Nchu and Mdantsane, but in both cases considerable support was given by state officials whose time was not costed.

The institutional and political context can be complex, as in Mgwali, and state officials do not generally seem keen to drive through incomplete or stalled processes. This is a similar problem to restitution. Full survey and planning are also needed prior to upgrading.

ULTRA remains an enabling Act that allows individuals or families to take responsibility for upgrading their own properties that are already surveyed. The Act requires careful amendment to clarify where it is applicable and to provide for family ownership. Some commentators see ULTRA as too difficult to implement and unsuitable for rural communal contexts because it extends private, titled landownership. We will discuss this issue in the following chapter and then examine alternative proposals.

5

Arguments for and against titling

GIVEN THAT ULTRA IS IN PLACE, and that it could be extended, what are the arguments for and against upgrading? Private tenure with title registered in the Deeds Office is an effective system of ensuring secure land rights. Local intermediaries or collectivities such as government officials, chiefs, CPA committees or communities would not have discretion to remove land from individuals or families with title.

Private titles are subject to public conditions of many kinds, especially but not only in urban areas, required by planning and zoning laws. They are subject to expropriation in certain legally specified contexts, but with compensation. Thus there are general restrictions on the use of private land. However, title provides one of the most secure forms of tenure, and this is a major argument for gradually making it universal. It would end the racially based dualism in South African landholding that has so long been highlighted by those critical of segregation and apartheid. Their aims have largely been achieved by the abolition of Acts that restricted access to private land, but the dualism remains and the off-register areas may be expanding.

Owners of land are more likely to qualify for mortgages and loans, which enable them to improve their properties and increase their value or, in the rural areas, to invest in agricultural equipment and production. Lack of capital and credit is a major constraint on investment in agriculture and on smallholder production more generally.

Deborah James illustrates in detail the expanding mortgage markets in South Africa.[37] There are of course downsides to this process in that it creates widespread indebtedness in a country with relatively high interest rates and high levels of debt. Moreover, mortgages and loans are made on the assumption that in the last resort lenders can take possession of a property for resale.

Urban township properties and RDP houses are already widely available for sale by means of formal channels through estate agents supported by lenders. Small rural properties in communal districts or urban properties in informal settlements are not worth as much and are less attractive to lending institutions, which may not be prepared to take the risk. Thus we should be cautious about exaggerating the value of titles for mortgages – at least initially – in such areas. Nevertheless, in some contexts, closer to the metros or in valuable agricultural areas, credit may be available.

Owners with title can sell their properties. In general, property prices have risen strongly in South Africa over recent decades and property owners are in a privileged position to accumulate.

During the apartheid era, black people were not only prevented from purchasing property in many parts of the country, but could not purchase property even in the African townships. This prohibition on African urban landownership during most of the apartheid era was a particularly short-sighted policy that had devastating results for the personal wealth of many African families – a hidden aspect of racial discrimination that inhibited social mobility and the formation of a middle class. This prohibition has of course now been removed in the cities but it remains intact in the former homelands, and on CPA land, where perhaps 35–40 per cent of African people still live and where many have landholdings. We have mentioned the scale of mobility in South Africa. If a family wishes to move from the countryside to the city, they cannot easily sell their property and they tend to arrive in the towns with little. This fuels urban informal settlements and insecurity. Of course, many families or individuals who move to town may choose to keep their rural landholdings. In some cases, African individuals or families hold private property in urban areas and customary rights in their rural homes.

In her paper for this project, entitled 'A home of their own', Khumisho Moguerane illustrates that black South African women with some resources, not all middle class, value the security of a home, and particularly a private home owned in their own name.[38] Such assets are not subject to the whims of male family members or of traditional authorities. Two of the women she interviewed were in fact dispossessed by chiefs at some point of their housing biographies. With private property they feel that they can establish a secure base for themselves and their families and can gradually invest in buildings. They see this as providing both security and status for the long term. Such women may be having a significant impact on the housing market in South Africa.

There is growing evidence of sales in customary/PTO areas. In theory, the improvements are being sold, not the land itself. Constraints on sale and the insecurity of tenure depress prices. The evidence of the scale of rural land markets is limited. Debbie Budlender found 8 per cent of women interviewed in a survey of 3,000 in rural villages acquired their sites through purchase.[39] The percentage may be higher if men are interviewed or in peri-urban areas and informal settlements. Hannah Dawson, researching in Zandspruit, found shacks are leased, bought and sold on some scale in this informal settlement.[40] Much depends on whether suitable land can still be acquired in other ways.

Without private property, land accumulation is very difficult. One of the major constraints on smallholder farming is the small size of arable plots, generally below 2 ha. The majority of rural families do not use their arable plots.[41] While many would prefer to hang onto these rights in land, some may relinquish them if they could gain income.

Hay and Mushwana illustrate in their paper on Limpopo for this project that at present those who wish to expand agricultural activity can generally do so by loaning land. De la Hey and Beinart found similarly that even in a Transkei rural village with high rainfall, there was little competition for arable fields, which could be accessed through family or other villagers for little or no payment. But leasing in this way is insecure and enables only annual crops to be grown during the season when animals are kept away.

Cultivators cannot fence or diversify crops, and this pattern restricts the incentives to invest. Long-term and year-round private control of arable plots is necessary if smallholders are to invest in agriculture and water supplies. The literature on links between tenure and smallholder production in Africa is large and not conclusive. There are many other factors involved, but in a recent survey Fenske found constraints on investment and diversification into tree crops where tenure is less secure.[42]

These are arguments for titling, and interviews in a number of rural districts suggest that people believe they own their land and use local vernacular words with something like that meaning. In Bizana people said that they were nailed to their land. By contrast, a number of academics and activists both in South Africa and beyond see titling as very likely to disadvantage poor people, and as unworkable. The central argument, ironically, concerns tenure security. While titling may give owners strong rights to their land, the ability to sell makes them vulnerable.

Poor families could be tempted to sell because even the relatively low prices that can be obtained for rural properties may seem to them a significant short-term benefit. They may be desperate for cash for immediate needs such as food and children's education. A recent study of two villages in the Eastern Cape found that food insecurity remained a significant problem for the poorest families.[43] For families dependent largely on a government grant such as a pension, for example, R50,000 for a rural site may represent nearly three years of income. Yet the longer-term value could be far greater, protected under a customary or PTO system in which they would retain rights for the future.

In the past, black private landowners have found themselves vulnerable to debt and the repossession of their property.[44] The remit of the *Jaftha* judgment, which may constrain such outcomes, is not yet clear.

Privatisation of an increasing amount of rural land would also probably increase the costs of gaining access. At present, it is possible to apply for a residential plot from a headman or a village committee for a single payment that may range from R60 plus the costs of a ceremony if the applicant is a local person to R1,500 if he or she is an outsider. These are generally one-off payments. If accumulators were able to buy plots, this might mean that others have to rent, as many do in the urban and peri-urban areas. However, there is still adequate space in the great majority of rural settlements to enable new allocations.

The question is where the greatest danger lies to off-register rights. Is it in looser customary rights that are not easy to defend against those with local political power, allied to external investors? Most of the cases of dispossession, or exclusion from development opportunities, seem to result from such scenarios of accumulation within the customary system. This echoes experiences reported from Ghana.[45] Or is the danger in a land market where wealthy accumulators may be able to buy out poor landholders for relatively small amounts? There is no simple answer and much depends on specific local contexts and the resources at stake.

There are, however, more complex scenarios. A poor rural family may be able to sell a rural plot, and move to another rural area where they can obtain a land allocation, or move to a more suitable urban context, where they could apply for a subsidised urban RDP house. The latter strategy may be more valuable to them in the short term, because it is easier to find employment, and in the longer term, because demand for housing tends to be stronger in the urban areas. However, the waiting lists for RDP houses are often long, and the family are more likely to end up as renters in a shack settlement.

The costs of owning private land is generally higher, in that it incurs rates and local taxes. In the former homelands, many African people who work in towns prefer to live on customary land because these costs are lower. Thus there is a noted thickening of settlement in areas of customary landholding near towns and transport routes. For example, thousands of residential sites are clustered around the road towards the Mtamvuna Bridge in former Transkei because it is a convenient place to settle for employment and services in southern KwaZulu-Natal. The same applies to large areas north of Pretoria within the old communal areas of Bophuthatswana.

A further argument against titling is that it is unworkable. Even if the state pays the initial costs of upgrading under ULTRA, the cost of subsequent transactions in private land is too high in relation to the value of sites and properties in most rural areas and informal settlements. Thus families sell properties off-register and fail to keep title deeds up to date. RDP houses are a case in point.[46]

Rosalie Kingwill argues that African families with long-established freehold tenure do not essentially operate as private individual owners in that they tend not to sell land but retain it as family property in which a number of people have rights. In effect, a customary system is partly overlaid on private land and she argues that it would be more effective to reflect this reality in legislation for a hybrid system of land administration.[47] In some cases where individually named owners have tried to sell properties, there has been a backlash by other family members who considered that they had informal rights in the properties. Nevertheless, such properties can legally be sold and disposed of.

Title-holders value their documents but do not generally keep them up to date. There is legislative provision in the Land Titles Adjustment Act of 1993 for the Registrar of Deeds to appoint a commissioner to update title deeds and to cover the costs of this procedure. This could not be done, however, on a large scale over the long term.

It is difficult to register the layered rights found in most

African rural contexts. Residential property and adjacent gardens are the most amenable to titling but do not represent the totality of landholdings. Arable land is usually situated at some distance from the homestead, rather than within a bounded farm, and in some villages the fields are still available for communal grazing after the harvest.

Rights to communal grazing and areas of bush are available to all local landholders and provide valuable resources to poor rural people. It would be difficult to reflect such differential rights in a title deed with its requirement for survey and strict boundaries.

Communal grazing has been privatised in parts of Africa, such as Machakos in Kenya, with some success, and this has led to an intensification of production because farmers could invest more securely in the land.[48] But privatisation of communal land would require a major reorganisation of settlements in African rural communities in South Africa.

Registration and upgrading also assume a neutral state and officials who will act in the interests of all landholders. Yet corruption has seeped into many state institutions and practices in South Africa. The danger of a large-scale titling exercise is that those with more power will be able to turn the exercise to their advantage and those with less power, even within families, notably women, may lose out.

In the past, women were disadvantaged in customary systems. However, customary systems are gradually enabling women to hold land independently of men.[49] Even in a relatively isolated area such as Amadiba in Bizana, former Transkei, women talked of owning land, and a senior local councillor said that customary law had changed in such a way as to allow landholdings by widows and unmarried women with children.[50]

The Department of Rural Development and Land Reform has recently published a bill in which it plans to undertake a major campaign of titling (see Appendix). Whether it has the capacity or commitment for this is unclear. If it is to be done as a single national campaign in favour of individual landholders, it is likely to be resisted by chiefs and others with a stake in the existing patterns of landholding. The department is proposing titling with a greater variety of potential outcomes.

There are clearly unpredictable gains and losses, both for economic development overall and for different groups of people, in such an initiative. Yet it is important to legislate for the future. Overall the trend seems to be towards claims of ownership and a more active housing and land market even in the rural areas. This reflects the scale of individual mobility. Many people want to move. On the whole, the strongest form of tenure is likely to be the most secure and it is possible to introduce conditions in titles that constrain sale.

6

Tenure and land administration

A hybrid route forward? A Land Records Act or more flexible titling?

As early as 1999, Martin Adams, who worked in President Nelson Mandela's Department of Land Affairs, remarked that the existing land administration system was breaking down:

> In each of the former homelands, land is administered by different laws and authorities. Generally, the systems of administration and record keeping have broken down and threaten a general collapse in rural governance. This collapse includes loss of records, doubts as to which laws apply and the unauthorised issue of permits and other documents.[51]

As we have noted, there is still no overarching, national land administration framework for off-register landholdings. Although these duties logically fall under the Department of Rural Development and Land Reform, or the Department of Co-operative Governance, responsibilities and systems have not been adequately developed.

Local customary arrangements and traditional councils continue to operate, sometimes with the assistance of government officials, but without formal authority to administer and regulate land rights in such a way that would complement and coexist with the present system of deeds registration.

Insecurity of tenure is thus compounded by the post-1994 weakness of land administration. The incoherence of the legislative and executive responses to the Constitution following IPILRA and the initial suite of defensive legislation has produced a confused legal and policy position. Some old-order legislation has remained on the statute books, but some of these laws are only applicable to ex-homelands, some are unenforceable, and some moribund.

Siyabu Manona, Rosalie Kingwill and others suggest a new system of land administration that gives strong rights to families who hold off-register land.[52] They argue that titles are unsuitable and that attempts to legislate for communal land rights have failed. The legislation now on the table favours traditional authorities and collective rights with limited protection for landholders. They believe that major legislation is required in the shape of a Land Records Act.

This would entail a statutory recording of all off-register rights. The proposed system could also incorporate freehold titles and quitrent rights which have fallen out of step with the Deeds Registry system. The proposed land records system should be parallel to Deeds Registry, located in the same government department and also articulate with it, so that there can be movement both ways. People should be able to upgrade to title if families agree. But some landholders are moving to a less formal system by default – as indicated by the informal sale of RDP houses without registering this with the Deeds Office.

The processes of clarifying rights are the first step towards protecting them. Simultaneously, the Act should provide for an administrative system for all valid claims to rights that are currently off-register. These should not be second-class rights that are not comparable in gravity to title deeds. It is suggested that the recording of rights could be done alongside a census. One central problem for a process of recording off-register land is the lack of detailed survey. In such contexts, which are common in developing countries, the International Federation of Surveyors advocates the recording of general boundaries as opposed to boundaries that must be surveyed with precision.

For those outside the profession, and especially those who have limited literacy, the concept of visual boundaries is sometimes better understood. While land surveyors may argue that these systems should not exist side by side, the proposed Land Records Act should accommodate both, allowing for progressive changes over time.

Where recorded rights are contested, they should go to a land rights inquiry or adjudication process. Disputes should not be heard initially by courts of law. The development of an effective system of adjudication will be a major element of the new law, and officials will have to be trained and their skills developed to ensure that this is effective.

The institution of a National Land Ombud could be a crucial vehicle for overseeing land rights and providing assistance to landholders. This institution would complement the proposed Land Records Act. An Ombud office would have powers to investigate state departments and to require compliance and action from them. This official would also investigate requests from individual members of the public and from organisations.

This proposal for a Land Records Act aims at an effective system that would record and develop strong rights for all off-register landholders in South Africa – who are probably the majority of landholders. It would work with defensive legislation – such as IPILRA and PIE – and protect rights at the level of families, not broader collectivities. It would be relatively inexpensive for poor landholders.

Such an Act, its proponents argue, could provide the basis for major new initiatives in planning and investment in the former homelands and in informal settlements, where some of the poorest South Africans live. It should potentially fit in with the Spatial Planning and Land Use Management Act 16 of 2013 (SPLUMA). SPLUMA is now the primary planning legislation for the whole of South Africa. It does not give land rights, but in order for SPLUMA to be implemented, landholders in the relevant area must have recognised rights.[53]

A Land Rights Act would provide a vehicle for the extension of planning and services into areas where they are generally under-provided and where effective planning is being held up by lack of clear land rights. SPLUMA places emphasis on incremental upgrading in previously disadvantaged areas. Municipalities are asked to identify suitable zones, and the Act states that 'land development procedures must include provisions that accommodate access to secure tenure and the incremental upgrading of informal areas'. Municipalities should 'include provisions that permit the incremental introduction of land use management and regulation in areas under traditional leadership, rural areas, informal settlements, slums and areas not previously subject to a land use scheme'.

These provisions fit well with the proposed Land Records Act and do not require title and full survey before planning and provision of a full range of services. A phased introduction of both measures has the potential to accommodate existing social dynamics, customary practices and power relations, which conventional approaches tend to ignore.

This might permit flexibility in relation not only to tenure but also to building regulations, plot sizes and land use. For example, it may be difficult to remove people already in informal or rural settlements in order to establish regular plot sizes, and rigorous regulation may discriminate against and exclude poor families. It is critical that SPLUMA and the Land Records Act should enhance their rights and security rather than undermine them. The aim should be to diminish spatial inequality without enforcing systems that result in prohibitively high costs for both municipalities and communities. Thus administrative flexibility will be required in the process of legalising informal settlements and extending planning and services to densely settled rural zones. There are particular challenges to be met in communal or customary tenure areas.

We agree that the idea of a Land Records Act or similar legislation is both promising and innovative in recording off-register land rights; the country has gone backwards in this respect. However, some important issues must be adequately thought through before this path is taken.

Firstly, does the government have the capacity and the expertise to implement and administer an Act of this kind with its demands for full recording, updating and long-term adjudication and dispute settlement? The Department of Rural Development and Land Reform cannot at present cope with all of its current duties. Government will have to commit itself to creating a new section of the department with a substantial long-term budget. State capacity is a critical question in successful implementation, even if elements of tenure reform are outsourced.

Secondly, will this system replicate the problems experienced in extending the titling system? It may be cheaper for landholders but they would still have to report regularly on any changes to the registered landholding and landholders. The state would still be responsible for updating and adjudicating at least as many properties (over six million) as currently in the Deeds Registry and probably many more. Some of these holdings will be complex and multifaceted. No one knows exactly how many new properties would need to be registered.

Innovative electronic systems and careful coordination of all the agencies involved, including effective offices such as the Surveyor-General and Stats SA, may make a national register possible. But it is difficult to see sufficient financial and administrative commitment. The various agencies of state cannot at present cope with the relatively basic task of ensuring that all RDP houses have full and up-to-date titles.

Thirdly, the same issue would arise as in titling – the agencies involved would need to be scrupulously fair and uncorrupt to ensure that local power-holders do not benefit from the process of registration. The proposed recording for a Land Records Act is dependent largely on state officials. But the involvement of professional groupings, such as conveyancers and surveyors, and a well-established Deeds Office may make private ownership less susceptible.

Fourthly, whatever the intention, a separate register may well be considered as second-best and could hamper integration of tenure into a single national system.

Perhaps it would be possible to take some of the innovative thinking around the Land Records Act and work this into a system of titling that may be sufficiently flexible to deal with the complexities of the African-occupied rural areas and to integrate them into a single national system. This alternative may not be as inclusive as a Land Records Act but we will discuss some ideas here.

The Deeds Registry is already well established and generally well run with experienced officials. The system of titles gives the strongest rights. The danger of a parallel and cheaper system may be to dilute the legal rigour and standing of the existing practices and laws around private property. Thus gradual, incremental extension of the existing, formal system of survey and titling may be the most satisfactory solution. This would require, in the first instance, major commitment to funding an expanded Deeds Office with well-trained staff and possibly more branches. It could not be a rapid process although it should be prioritised in the department. And this route would put a premium on improving existing protective legislation for off-register landholders.

The Department of Rural Development and Land Reform, the Deeds Office and the other agencies involved need to address urgently the backlog of issuing titles for RDP housing and any outstanding upgrading exercises. Commitment to initial costs of survey and registration, and subsidy for transfer of properties below a certain price, may help to diminish informalisation of transfers; and this could also be a more effective strategy than an entirely new land records system.

Similarly, the Land Titles Adjustment Act of 1993 is available to update existing private property registered with the Deeds Office, and resources could be put into this. The question is whether sufficient incentives exist to ensure a growing commitment to the formal system over the long term. The key probably lies in costs and in the market for properties – a conviction by both buyers and sellers that value will be better maintained if full, formal land rights are secured.

GPS systems, computerised recording of titles and availability of information on the web, and thus via cellphone, may greatly reduce costs both of initial registrations and later transactions. This may all also assist in the expansion of cheaper estate agent, survey and conveyancing costs. Established institutions and professions such as mortgage providers, conveyancers, surveyors and estate agents are all invested in the existing system and have – to varying degrees – an interest in extending it. They also have well-developed training systems and professional codes. These professional bodies may find some interest in and commitment to assisting in a national programme that significantly expands titling – although they too need careful regulation so that consultants and private-sector interests do not take advantage of state resources.

As noted above, critics of titling argue that it is insufficiently flexible to cope with the notions of family rights that underpin African concepts of ownership. Consideration could be given to a form of family title that would recognise the rights of more people than simply an individual owner. There are already a number of different forms of joint ownership or co-ownership of immovable property, including community of property, partnership and undivided shares, as well as trust and company ownership.

Undivided co-ownership entitles named owners to a share of the whole property. In general, the commonly held property may not be divided, or encumbered or alienated, without the consent of the other co-owners. These provisions may already give sufficient flexibility to meet the needs of African family ownership. However, it would also be possible to develop an amendment to the existing law that caters for a more flexible form of family ownership. Again, this strategy could be contained within the existing system of registration and professional practice. Under the Deeds Registry Act, conveyancers take responsibility for accurately describing and recording the property and for consulting and reaching consent about disposal and transactions (section 15A).

Family ownership could also be a significant factor in reducing alienation of land by poor owners because sale would require wider consent and thus make property more 'sticky' if the owners so required. Conditions on title relevant to this issue, such as restrictions on alienability for debt, may reinforce family control. We do not know enough about the legal position to suggest further conditions, such as inalienability at least for a period. The state was apparently able to put this condition on RDP titles.

However, we should mention a few caveats. Firstly, by no means all African owners will want family control, especially of urban properties. This issue may be of more relevance to rural homesteads, where land is inherited rather than purchased and 'living customary law' can be brought to bear.

Secondly, relations within families are not without conflict. Deciding who to include with an undivided or family share is open to contestation. In a changing social context where, as Moguerane notes, individual women are seeking more independent control over property, many owners may not wish to burden their property rights with multiple owners. We should distinguish between formal ownership rights in landholdings and more informal customary social expectations of mutual support and generosity. For example, generosity and hospitality can be shown to siblings, children and grandchildren without including them in formal ownership of property. Ownership would also allow property to be bequeathed to specific beneficiaries rather than simply inherited.

Urban and peri-urban landholdings without arable fields or grazing rights clearly fit more easily into the Deeds Office system than rural landholdings. However, an increasing number of rural sites are also without fields. And it would be possible to expand title to specific components of rural residential landholdings without threatening the others. For example, rural residential and garden plots, many of them now in village settlements and bounded by fences, could easily be surveyed and titled without restricting broader claims to rights in commonages. This was done in the nineteenth-century Eastern Cape for white and black settlements, before the Glen Grey Act. Villages were laid out with private tenure over residential sites and arable fields while missions or village management boards managed the common areas. Rights over commonage could be written into title deeds. Alternatively, commonages could be subdivided – as was done when some of the white-owned settlements were upgraded. Upgrading and registration need not preclude further allocation of residential sites on the commonage. This would be important in ensuring that some land remains accessible at low cost.

Officials in the Department of Rural Development and Land Reform have been thinking on the same lines in some recent policy documents.[54] A paper on communal land tenure policy, probably from 2014, talks of ensuring that household land rights are 'formalized as individual title-holders'. A little confusingly, it continues to say that these should be institutionalised-use rights. But the rights described will be perpetual and bequeathable. This has clearly been debated within the department. A version of a new Communal Land Rights Bill circulated in 2016 seemed to lay more emphasis on collective control under traditional councils and CPAs. The latest version, published in July 2017, is – as we will explain in the Appendix – potentially flexible and envisages that communities choose between private ownership for individuals and collective ownership.

These suggestions about an extension of upgrading and titling do not adequately meet the administrative problems discussed, but they will gradually diminish the need for a separate administrative system for off-register land.

7

Registration and spatial reorganisation

THE SPATIAL ORGANISATION of African rural settlements also impacts on tenure debates and the possibilities for upgrading. The layout of many African rural settlements, especially on the eastern side of the country, was changed when betterment and rehabilitation schemes were imposed from the 1940s to the 1980s. This applied both to new settlements created under the 'Native Trust' and many, although not all, older settlements.

Homesteads were clustered into villages so that services could potentially be extended. The size of residential plots varied in different areas from about 0.1 ha to 0.25 ha. These villages were generally considered agricultural villages, so provision was made in the plots for livestock kraals and gardens. In denser settlements, plots were smaller. Arable lands, generally up to 2 ha, were sited away from the main villages. Where planning was done effectively, these fields were demarcated on suitable soil and carefully contoured to minimise soil erosion.

The rest of the land around the villages was pasture and

an attempt was made to introduce fences around the camps to enable rotational grazing and to protect the fields. Ideally the livestock could be left out during the nights in order to minimise damage to the veld. With some limited exceptions, fenced camps have failed in the former homeland areas.

The legacy of betterment has resulted in some major problems. Most African rural landholders do not have farms in the sense that they can consolidate their landholdings around their homesteads. It is also difficult for rural landholders to expand their landholdings around their homesteads because they are clustered in villages. Some on the edges of villages are able to extend their gardens, and there are also a few examples of people moving out of the villages and back onto the commonage.[55]

The arable fields are usually grouped together and are seldom fenced. This means they cannot easily be protected from animals.[56] When livestock were carefully herded, they could be kept away for the growing season and then, after the harvest, let loose onto the fields to graze maize stubble and deposit manure. Lack of labour for herding makes this difficult and damage to crops by livestock is one reason that most fields are not now being used. A critical question for the future of the African rural areas and the country as a whole is whether these arable fields (or other parts of the commonage) can be brought back into production.

As our research in both Limpopo and the Eastern Cape indicates, it is generally possible for prospective farmers to get access to a few hectares of arable land but it is difficult to establish exclusive, year-round control of fields.

Experiments with spatial reorganisation may be valuable alongside tenure reform. One strategy would be to facilitate farms on the arable lands. If these were upgraded to ownership, then accumulators may be able to gain control of a few fields, fence them and invest in them.

In parts of Kenya, such as Machakos, pasture land has also been subdivided to make individually held farms.[57] Livestock are to a greater degree stall-fed. It is unlikely that many communities would agree to this in South Africa, but it is certainly worth thinking about. If, for example, 300 homesteads were sited in a village with 300 ha of demarcated arable land and another 5,000 ha of pasture land, then it would be possible to consolidate roughly 100 holdings of 50 ha by sale and purchase.

An alternative is already evident where communities effectively lease their arable land to projects. This is being done, for example, by the Fort Hare dairy scheme in Annshaw, near Middledrift, Eastern Cape.[58] It is an area of privately held African land, and this large-scale enterprise has planted and irrigated pastures on about fifty former arable fields.

In Willowvale, a macadamia nut scheme has been started on 300 ha of village land. This kind of project is also evident on some CPA land after restitution; in these cases, such as fruit farms in the Levubu valley, Limpopo, the CPAs have generally taken over existing concerns.[59] Although 'strategic partnerships' have met with mixed results, in principle they enable well-capitalised external agencies to develop joint enterprises on communal land and for the landholders to gain a share, either through rental income to the individual landholders or through a transfer of profits to a representative body. Our aim here is not to evaluate strategic partnerships but to argue that clearly defined property rights are essential in such cases so that families can ensure their share.

8

The courts and the protection of family rights in customary systems[60]

LEGISLATION AND ADMINISTRATIVE systems are key routes for developing tenure security for those with off-register rights. However, the courts have also made judgments that potentially give guidance to legal developments in these areas.

The Constitutional Court in particular has been concerned with protecting socio-economic rights for disadvantaged people and communities. The areas where off-register rights predominate include people who are among the poorest in South Africa, and it is important that their rights are not shouldered aside. Although many people invest a great deal in their houses on these sites, sometimes in villages with few services, the form of tenure does not seem very conducive to investment in agriculture. In certain respects the areas under these communalist forms of tenure are expanding through restitution and redistribution. It is thus all the more important to clarify landholding rights both in the older customary/ PTO areas and in the new CPAs.

Our main concern in this chapter is to explore and analyse a few cases in which the courts have contributed to define or modify forms of customary, non-private tenure and in this sense have been indirectly engaged in the process of tenure reform. They have done so with reference to legislation and the Constitution but not explicitly with reference to policy developments, and perhaps not in any planned way. They have done so both 'positively', through clarifying and in some respects redefining customary tenure, and 'negatively', through declaring the Communal Land Rights Act of 2004 unconstitutional.

We ask whether these judgments can form the basis for stronger individual and family rights, and a form of ownership to specific pieces of residential and arable land. The main reference point is three cases in the former Transkei in which landholders were deprived of their land or threatened with this.

The key judgment by the Constitutional Court in this respect was in *Alexkor* vs *Richtersveld Community* (2003) – a case contested to resolve issues that arose under the implementation of the Restitution of Land Rights Act of 1994. The court accepted the restitution claim by the community over an area that had been appropriated for mining during the 1920s. But they went further in describing the nature of the community's rights to that land. The court was guided by the need to reinterpret the significance of 'indigenous' or customary law because this was recognised by the Constitution. They were obliged to apply it when appropriate and when it was not at odds with the provisions and values of the Constitution. *Richtersveld*, as the case was called, opened up the possibility that all communal or customary land in South Africa was held under a form of ownership. The judges talked of the form of rights and occupation as being 'akin to that held under common-law ownership'.

They concluded: 'We have found that the Richtersveld Community held ownership of the subject land under indigenous law.' While they did not specifically use the term 'communal indigenous ownership', it was being circulated within a couple of years. This approach had been developed by the Legal Resources Centre (with Henk Smith as attorney and Wim Trengrove as advocate in the case) with the express intent of trying to strengthen the customary rights held by communities in land.

The strength of land rights held by families in communal or customary tenure was one of the central issues in two land restitution cases in Bizana district, Mpondoland, Eastern Cape. Both were long-running land claims made in 1995. Both proved difficult to settle, partly because of conflict between the parties involved and partly because the Eastern Cape Land Restitution Commission did not seem to have the capacity to take a strong lead.

In *Hlolweni et al.* vs *North Pondoland Sugar* (hearing 2009 and judgment 2010), 883 claimants were awarded 10,000 ha that had been appropriated by the former Transkei government around 1980 to establish a sugar plantation and sugar smallholder scheme within the homeland. This case was decided by Judge Fikile Bam, Judge President of the Land Claims Court, with Alan Dodson, who had long experience in land cases, as the lead advocate for the community. Judge Bam considered that the *Richtersveld* case set a precedent and confirmed that the claimant communities had 'communal indigenous ownership' over the land. Their claim to the land overrode any rights that the Transkei government may have asserted, and also by implication negated the power of the paramount chief and local chief to alienate such land without the consent of the communal indigenous owners.

The *Mgungundhlovu* case was settled by the judge and the parties in 2014 shortly after the site inspections, but before the case proper had begun (in the Ebenezer Church hall, Elurholweni). Here a community of 106 claimants, represented by Dodson and others, were awarded about 740 ha that had been taken over by the Transkei government at the same time and leased to the company that built and ran the Wild Coast Sun casino and hotel. The settlement, recognised by a court order, was particularly favourable, giving the claimants ownership of all the land they had lost, rental income and a share of the enterprise.

The 2010 *Hlolweni* judgment was an affirmation of that made in the *Richtersveld* case, but there were significant differences. *Richtersveld* restored land to an undifferentiated group or community of Nama/coloured people. The whole community regained rights over the area of land taken by the government in the 1920s and mined by the Alexkor Company. The judgment did not differentiate between chiefs and people, or identify any subset of claimants within that community. Individual claimant families did not have to show that they had occupied the land before the 1920s or that they had specific rights to the land that was appropriated. The whole of the Richtersveld community gained communal indigenous ownership over the whole of the alienated land – even though it was only a portion of the area recognised as their historical land.

In the *Hlolweni* case, the claimant community was not a whole undifferentiated group of Imizizi (the local chieftaincy) or a larger Mpondo chiefdom, but a list of about 883 families who had been specifically dispossessed by the alienation of the land. The judgment was in favour of the specific group of claimants. Judge Bam in certain respects refined the content of communal indigenous ownership to mean a particular set of people rather than an indigenous community identified by their ethnicity as a whole.

In both *Hlolweni* and *Mgungundhlovu*, chiefs at various levels had cooperated with the Transkeian state in agreeing to the alienation of land and the forcible removal of people who had previously occupied it. In both cases, Botha Sigcau, who was simultaneously President of Transkei, Paramount Chief or King of Eastern Mpondoland, and head of the Qaukeni regional authority had agreed to the alienation of the land. He also agreed to an even more sizeable alienation for the Magwa tea estates in Lusikisiki district (although fewer people were involved.) In the Imizizi case, Chief Mditshwa had tried to voice community opposition, but at Mgungundhlovu the amaDiba chief Baleni had agreed to the alienation and clearing of the land.

In the *Hlolweni* case, Judge Bam effectively ruled that the chiefs and former tribal authorities did not have the legal power to alienate land without the consent of those who had customary rights. It had to be shown in the court case that the community of individual claimants did not consent, and this was also expected to be a significant point in the *Mgungundhlovu* case.

These decisions are important for contemporary South Africa because chiefs are reasserting local authority, in parallel to democratic local government institutions, or claiming rights over land and development initiatives on behalf of communities. This includes attempts to alienate land held in customary tenure for purposes of development.

People now have legislative protection against removal

through IPILRA, which they did not have in 1980. However, as noted above, IPILRA may not have prevented the alienation of land of specific families if a majority of the community had agreed. In the *Hlolweni* judgment, and in the arguments presented for *Mgungundhlovu*, it was accepted that the community involved was the collectivity of affected landholders. They had strong rights to their land, which were akin to ownership. They had to be consulted and to give explicit consent if they were to be moved.

This same question may now be tested with respect to the removal of people at Xolobeni in Bizana for coastal mining. In this case too, it is critical that the community is not defined as a much broader ethnic or chiefly-led grouping.

Certain gains have been made from the recognition of this element of customary law and its redefinition by the courts. But there are also dangers. The most important concern is that the judgments tend to equate customary rights with collective ownership. The Constitutional Court judgment seemed to privilege an ethnically identified community. We believe that the law should not imply this, otherwise the idea of communal indigenous ownership may become the basis for a new local tribalism. Judge Bam's interpretation, restricting the idea to those directly affected by a removal, is more appropriate, but it still does not cater for family rights.

Although these issues were not tested in the *Mgungundhlovu* case, the 106 claimants asserted 'communal indigenous ownership'. Research established that the claimant families had lived in the alienated area. The claimants' legal team could show the actual location of the homesteads of many of those families, and in fact this was done for a few specific cases during the site inspection. The claim was on behalf of those families alone, and not the broader amaDiba chieftaincy or any other collective entity.

After the settlement in 2014, a CPA was formed. The Department of Rural Development and Land Reform wished to include the chief in the CPA, but the community successfully insisted on forming one independent of the chief. This is particularly important because the settlement was so favourable.

This same issue has bedevilled the resolution of the *Hlolweni* case. After judgment in 2010, the formation of a CPA was delayed till 2012 because of opposition by the chief (whose position was itself subject to dispute). By 2016, the land had not yet been transferred to the CPA for the same reason. Despite the clear judgment by the Judge President of the Land Court, the department delayed making the award to the CPA. This question needs urgently to be settled at the national level.

The issue is whether CPAs independent of chiefs can be formed within the former homelands. A judgment to this effect seems to have been made in 2015 (see below). However, the Eastern Cape provincial government, which has close links with regional chiefs, remained reluctant to act on the judgment in the *Hlolweni* case up to the time of our last visit in 2016. This large and valuable area remained unsettled and disputed, although it is being used for grazing and a couple of forestry projects.

The question remains as to exactly what communal indigenous or customary ownership means and whether it can be developed further.

The court judgments so far are potentially positive for restoring African customary land within the legal framework of the Restitution Act. They potentially reinforce IPILRA in providing protection for people who are threatened by removals and do not have written documentation to prove their land rights. They go a step further than IPILRA in specifying a positive right to land, akin to ownership, rather than simply a defence against removal. This right lies with a group of families and is good against chiefs, government or private interests.

However, these judgments are confusing for any upgrading of tenure. There is no clear direction within them that recognises rights of individual families to specific pieces of land. The named claimants in the cases reviewed achieved a collective right to the land as a community. Their ownership rights are vested in a CPA that will manage the whole area.

In the *Mgungundhlovu* settlement, the CPA was awarded the ownership of the 740 ha of land on which the Wild Coast Sun is sited as a whole. The claimants did not acquire rights to return to their own family holdings. About half of the area that was alienated is directly occupied by the casino, hotel and golf course. These will continue to operate. The claimant community was awarded shares in the casino and the right to rental from the Wild Coast Sun. But they cannot use this land as individuals.

They have also accepted restrictions on the use of the rest of the land for about twenty years. This precludes the return of individual families to most of the rest of the land. It is unlikely that the CPA would agree to the return of any families to their old lands because it would be so unfair to the many who cannot return. The CPA intends to manage the whole of the land for the benefit of the claimants.

Thus 'communal indigenous ownership' and the reinforcement of customary ownership do not yet seem to establish the right of individual families to individual pieces of land. The same applies to CPAs more generally, which are created to take ownership of farms that are not customary land. The CPAs can allocate land but at present they do not assign ownership over individual plots. Perhaps this has been implied and perhaps the concept could be extended to protect a single family or individual claim. Perhaps there have been cases of restitution where individual families have returned to their old sites on land held in customary tenure.

Some further issues arise. Do these rulings, by relying on the idea of *communal* indigenous ownership, give all the descendants of the claimant families a right? In Richtersveld, for example, will anyone accepted into the community be entitled to use the land? Will the number of individuals entitled to a share in the Mgungundhlovu CPA continue to increase? Are communities infinitely expandable? This is one of the major problems of restitution settlements and CPAs as a whole – and potentially of the idea of communal indigenous ownership.

Judgments in some restitution cases (see below) have narrowed the definition of communities. But they have not clearly circumscribed inheritance. In practice, it may be the case that most descendants will lose interest in the land, but this aspect of collective rights needs to be clarified.

A further question arises as to which African settlements are held in this form of ownership? Does this term apply only to those who can show they are descendants of long-established families or ethnic groups?

By contrast, IPILRA seems to recognise a defence against removal after five years. Those removed from their land in Hlolweni and Mgungundhlovu generally found other smaller sites, crammed in among neighbouring settlements or excised from communal pasturage. Their new sites were smaller, often less favourable, and they often comprised only residential plots with small gardens. Have they established secure communal indigenous ownership in the 35 years in their new places? It would be hugely unfair if such families, who have already been forcibly removed, were not secure on their new sites. What are the tests?

In the *Richtersveld* case, evidence was led to show deep historical occupation and ownership because it had to be proved that the community held the land before the 1920s. The Constitutional Court also ruled that annexation did not override communal indigenous ownership. Research for *Mgungundhlovu* similarly showed that the annexation of Mpondoland in 1894 did not remove land rights.

Oral evidence demonstrated that some of the families in the claimant community had been in occupation for over a century. But the courts or the government need to clarify the timeframes essential in establishing customary ownership and whether it applies with the same force to recent incomers who are granted sites but who may not have any historical connection. Does IPILRA imply a five-year rule for customary ownership? Is the process of allocation relevant?

It is time to strengthen definitively the land rights of individuals and families. We have illustrated strategies for doing this by legislation and administrative reform. The Constitutional Court itself can surely go further than it has done so far in order to meet the expectations of the Constitution in section 25. This will depend on a number of contingencies: the right case, as well as judges who are prepared to use the Constitution creatively and move the interpretation of section 25 forward to entrench individual and family rights. Is there no mechanism through which the court can make a declaration about the strength of family rights under customary law being akin to ownership?

There have been further judgments suggesting that the courts tend to rule in favour of the rights of ordinary people, particularly in relation to the state and chiefs. In the *Bakgatla* case (2015), a CPA of claimants was formed in the North West Province to take control of restituted land.[61] It was common cause that the community was forcibly removed to make way for a game reserve during the apartheid era. But the Bakgatla Tribal Authority and Kgosi Pilane had interceded with the Department of Rural Development and Land Reform and disputed the constitution of the CPA as a community association that was not controlled by the chieftaincy. Because of this dispute, the department had only granted a temporary CPA and had tried unsuccessfully to arbitrate between the claimants and the chief. The department then refused to renew the CPA.

The Constitutional Court accepted that the temporary, provisional CPA had not ceased to exist and they placed the responsibility for its failure on the Director-General. They recognised that the community had gone through the correct process to establish the CPA, with extensive meetings and consultation.

In the judgment (with Chief Justice Mogoeng and Deputy Chief Justice Moseneke), the court agreed that they had jurisdiction because the case fell within the ambit of section 25 of the Constitution. Furthermore, they accepted that customary practices should be interpreted within the overall aims of the Constitution to secure equal rights, for example in respect of women: 'The [CPA] Act seeks to transform customary law and bring it in line with the Constitution. At the same time, the Act extends the fruits of democracy to traditional communities that are still subject to customary law. This is the context in which these provisions must be read and understood.' The court interpreted this to mean that the claimant community had the right to establish the CPA without the chief.

In many respects, this judgment echoed and reinforced that of Judge Bam in the *Hlolweni* case, where the assumption was made that the beneficiaries of a restitution claim could constitute themselves as a legal community. It did not rule that chiefs and traditional councils could not participate in CPAs, because a community had the freedom to constitute itself in this way, but it went further than the specific point of law to promote an interpretation that the 'claimants [should have] the fullest possible protection of their constitutional guarantees'.

All things being equal, the court ruled that the Constitution prefers modification of customary law towards universal equal rights and towards a democratic dispensation at the local level. 'Where a traditional community or the majority of its members, as was the position in this case, have chosen the democratic route contemplated in the Act, effect must be given to the wishes of the majority …[By] effecting registration, the Department would be creating a platform for democracy to flourish among the Bakgatla ba Kgafela Traditional Community.'

The Constitutional Court's 2013 judgment in *Pilane and Another* struck down a set of interdicts obtained by a senior traditional leader prohibiting meetings of certain community members in the Bakgatla ba Kgafela area. The *Pilane* judgment held that the use of interdicts by traditional leaders to ban meetings or gatherings of dissidents violates the latter's constitutional rights to freedom of expression, association and assembly. The court delivered a clear message that the restraint of such rights was inappropriate and disquieting, especially in a constitutional democracy in which robust engagement should be favoured over litigation wherever possible. The court noted with disapproval the traditional leader's litigious record and 'lack of restraint' with regard to using legal tactics rather than engaging in meaningful dialogue, which could be seen as an attempt to silence criticism. The judgment was received as a major legal victory for constitutional freedoms in the face of the increasing assertion of chiefly power.

However, as in *Hlolweni*, the judgment has not always been followed, and traditional leaders continued to seek interdicts and other court orders to try to prevent meetings that they did not control. These problems are particularly heightened in traditional communities affected by mining or other developments where traditional leaders stand to benefit from lucrative deals.[62]

In a case about Cala (2015), in which Lungisile Ntsebeza, director of the African Studies Centre at the University of Cape Town, was an expert witness, the Eastern Cape High Court seems to have delivered a similar judgment. A headmanship in Cala fell vacant and the community claimed that they had always elected their headmen. The chief, supported by the provincial MEC, argued that whatever the past practice, the new Traditional Leadership and Governance Act of 2005, the Eastern Cape version of the national Act of 2003, gave the senior traditional leader and council this power.

The community argued that the Act in fact required that the customary practice and law of the specific area in which the headman was being appointed should be followed. Judge Plasket ruled that the 2003 Act does formalise traditional leadership but 'in accordance with the dictates of democracy in South Africa'. He was guided by key decisions, such as *Bhe* and *Richtersveld*, that acknowledged both the validity of elements of customary law and also the limitations placed on it by the Bill of Rights and the Constitution.

Judge Plasket accepted Ntsebeza's evidence that the headmanship had been elected for over a century and had passed between different families. Local election was consonant with the values of democratic governance and other fundamental political rights. The judge, however, recognised that the law may be applied differently across the province, making allowance for custom. This judgment is perhaps a little more ambivalent than in the *Bakgatla* case. Cala district is not unique in electing headmen over the long term. But the implication was that in districts where historically chiefs had more influence in the appointment of headmen, the 2005 provincial legislation could be interpreted differently.

Taken as a whole, these judgments indicate that the courts, and particularly the Constitutional Court, tend to support democratic rights and processes, and generally protect the interests of citizens against traditional authorities. However, the government has not always taken the same position nor always acted on court decisions. The specific question of family rights to their landholdings does not seem to have been the subject of a definitive judgment.

9

Tenure, land markets and production

A case study from Limpopo

IN THIS CHAPTER WE FOCUS on research by Hay and Mushwana for this project in the high-rainfall Mopani district, Limpopo. They investigated access to land, tenure security and the relationship between tenure and agricultural production.

In 2000 Lahiff had published a study of the Olifants-Arabie irrigation scheme in Limpopo. He found that while tribal authorities had the power to repossess land under certain circumstances 'outright dispossession is rare, and the communal system is generally seen as a reasonably secure form of tenure'.[63] He found people held the assumption that the land belonged to them and inheritance of land was recognised in practice. People sold or otherwise exchanged land informally on the scheme, framed in terms of selling the improvements on the land rather than the land itself. However, Lahiff, as well as Oomen, found that women, youths and outsiders struggled to get access to land independently in rural villages, although this was possible in dense settlements near towns.[64]

In 2016, Hay and Mushwana found a similar situation.[65] People generally perceived their tenure to be secure, stands were inherited and kept in the family, and people bought and sold land, as we discuss further below. However, it appeared easier for women and foreigners to access land in Mopani district by 2016. They found examples of women inheriting land, and also of single women accessing land independently.

Buying a stand from another person is a largely informal transaction. While many people will say that the land itself cannot be sold as it ultimately belongs to the chief, it is understood that the assets on the stand, specifically the house, are owned by the stand-holder. While the stand cannot be sold privately, a house can be. Thus, people looking for a house can negotiate directly with the house-owner, and not involve the headman or chief.

The stand, however, is transferred with the house and it is the stand-holder who benefits from the proceeds of the sale of his or her stand. These private transactions are enabled by the fact that it is possible to change the name of the registered stand-holder, by registering a 'change of ownership' with the headman. The new stand-holder will then receive an informal certificate, which is still called a PTO.

However, this part of the transaction is not always followed in that a 'change of ownership' is not always registered. Furthermore, the legal status of a PTO is uncertain. The cost of the houses varies dramatically, but even the highest amount a house can apparently reach is less than would generally be found in the urban private property market. The researchers heard of prices between R5,000 and R80,000. (A one-bedroom RDP house in Soweto would probably cost at least double that, but RDP houses are widely available for sale in less central parts of Gauteng for around R100,000.) Prices in Mopani are affected by size and design, state of services and the distance to a main road.

Generally, those who did not inherit stands from their parents, as well as outsiders, get access to land through headmen. Land is generally available for residential sites except in peri-urban areas or along main roads because historically the bulk of land in former homelands was reserved for communal grazing.

If a person is a local, then they can get land for a small payment of about R60. If the applicant is from outside, then a fee from R500 to R800 is expected for a residential site.[66] In a poorer, deep rural village one family had been given a stand for a fee of R150 – not yet paid.[67] There are no more costs to pay in rental because the perception is that the stand is now 'owned' by the stand-holder.

However, stand-holders are expected to pay a small yearly levy to the traditional authority, between R10 and R20. People are not directly forced to pay the levy, but a register is taken of all who have paid, and this is consulted whenever a person requires any service – for example, a reference letter to take to a potential employer, or a proof of residence certificate, which is required for getting a cell-phone contract, opening a bank account or acquiring an official document.

Plots for cultivation can be inherited. As with residential stands, the perception is that, once allocated, these plots belong to the plot-holder, and there is no yearly or monthly rental to pay. Historically, such plots were in short supply but the general withdrawal from arable production by smallholders means that it is now relatively easy to find land.

One elderly man said with regard to agricultural land, 'If you have got power you have permission to take whatever hectares you want. As long as you know you have the power to use it.' By power he meant the ability and resources to clear and cultivate the land, usually by tractor.[68] Another elderly man said that he could access land for free, and 'as long as we make the place clean, no problem'.[69]

Many people the researchers spoke to referred to their PTO as a 'deed of grant', which reflects the feeling that the stand is 'owned' by them. Changing the name of a stand-holder is referred to as a 'change of ownership' of the stand even by headmen and chiefs. In the language people use to describe their tenure, 'ownership' comes up frequently. As noted above, the same term is used in the rural Transkei.

No one felt their landholding was insecure. Asked directly if it would be possible for a chief to take away land, informants tended to answer, 'He won't.' Even the woman who had so far failed to pay R150 for her stand still felt reasonably secure: 'there's nothing that can happen, even if we don't pay they won't take our land. See all these places they were in the bush. They just cut the land and then people start building houses.'[70] Interviewees believed that if a landholder clears the vegetation, their claim is strengthened.

With regard to agricultural land the response was also that they felt secure, that it was unlikely they would one day find someone else cultivating their land, or have it taken away.

The idea that the act of clearing land, building on it and ploughing it is part of establishing 'ownership' has deep historical roots. Furthermore, the perception – and practice – is that once land has been allocated to a family, it is usually inherited by the youngest son when parents pass away, or if inheritance is not so straightforward, it still remains within the family.

There were nevertheless signs of insecurity which belied the confidence of respondents. Some did not have PTOs, and there were examples of people losing access to land that had been granted to them. For example, a respondent was given a new plot in a village a few years previously, but owing to lack of money had not yet built anything on the stand. She had access to a house in a different village, in which she could live for free, and so was not staying on the new stand. On a visit to her plot one day she found that someone else was using it. She approached the headman to complain and he initially could not remember the allocation. The headman's wife, however, was listening in on the conversation, and intervened, saying that he had in fact taken money for the site and allocated a stand. The headman referred to the principle that land can be reallocated if it was not being used. Nevertheless, the original allottee's right was recognised, and she and her partner erected a fence around their stand.

On a visit in July 2016, however, they found a neighbour had taken the fence down in order to extend her own plot. There was little they could do because in the absence of written rules and records, their rights to the land were uncertain. There is a loose understanding of customary tenure requiring use (use land or lose it), although this is not uniformly imposed. The fluid situation allowed people to pursue their interests, especially if they had strong local support.

In another example, the nephew of an elderly woman sold the stand and house she was living in to a buyer for cash. He did not consult his aunt and she only found out about the sale when she was told she would have to move. She went to see the chief, who declared the sale invalid as the nephew was not the registered stand-holder, and a change of ownership had not been registered. The chief also asserted his right over the land. In this instance, the aunt's tenure was protected and the purchaser lost his money as the nephew had already spent it.

There were a few other cases where chiefs protected the vulnerable. This example also highlights the insecurity of women when it comes to family property. The nephew's presumption that he could get away with selling the stand of his elderly aunt is reflective of gender and generational relationships within communal areas. It is still sometimes presumed that female children will leave their natal family home to live with their husbands and that men will inherit. This is a major motivation for women to have land allocated in their own right and, if possible, registered in their own names – a finding that echoes Khumisho Moguerane's discussion.[71]

A third example indicates the link between political authority and security of tenure. On valuable land close to a main road, authority was contested by the Maake and Nkuna traditional councils. Settlers acquired land through one chief, but the other chief insisted that the land in fact belonged to him and he had the houses bulldozed. After a court case the dispute was allegedly settled, and people began building again on this prime location, having approached the correct chief. A stand-holder who was overseeing a team of workers building his house there was very confident of his claim to the stand.

Tenure insecurity based on conflicting claims to land and uncertainty around authority over land is also pervasive in the context of land restitution. On a farm which was claimed by the Mokgolobotho community, near Tzaneen, Limpopo, many people have purchased stands and started building houses and cultivating. However, the CPA is in disarray, and the person responsible for allocating stands and taking payment for them does not have the support of the CPA or the community.

The rental market is very limited. In part this was because of the possibility of getting sites in many areas. Foreigners who are unable to get access to their own stands rent rooms where demand is higher in settlements near to employment opportunities and transport links. But renting out unused property in return for money was not common amongst interviewees.

One of the most surprising findings of this research was how common it is to cultivate someone else's land, to live in someone else's house or use someone else's property for a business, without paying anything. One respondent used an empty house belonging to an acquaintance to open a hairdressing salon and was not asked to pay any rent.[72] She and her partner similarly lived in the house of an acquaintance for free. Another used someone else's plot at Thabina Irrigation Scheme for free, because the original landholder 'has many others' and doesn't mind her using it.[73] A woman who was unsuccessful in getting the land she wanted for cultivation through a headman used part of a neighbour's residential stand.[74]

A common explanation given is that the land is not being used, the plot-holder does not need it, and is happy that their place is being looked after. But renting out property or land was also perceived as risky because of the perception that landholders should be using the land themselves and not have more than they needed.[75]

In Mopani district, leasing a plot without the chief's consent could result in problems if the lessee refuses to move. The only way to resolve such a dispute would be to go to the chief, and the chief may favour the occupant because they were using the plot. This may help to explain the preference that people seem to have for informal arrangements, rather than leasing land for cash.

People do not generally agree that chiefs 'own' the land

and, as noted, use the term of ownership for their own rights. But it is difficult to challenge those with local political power when disputes arise.

For example, a respondent wanted to begin farming commercially on a small scale but did not have access to land in the communal area in which she lived. She expressed her desire for land to a friend of hers, who happened to be the cousin of a chief in another part of the district. That chief allocated three hectares of land for them to cultivate.

They did well, approached the chief for more land, and were given 50 ha. However, this additional 50 ha could not be given to them through a PTO or customary allocation because the maximum allowed is seen to be about 5 ha. They had to pay the chief a high rent, allegedly of R1,000 per hectare, for an annual lease on the land, which left little room for profit.

A local NGO worker informed her that the chief did not own the land, but rather the land was owned by the state and that, as custodian, he could not demand rent. With this information, including a document showing that the land was state-owned, she approached the chief, who, after some disagreement, backed down. Rental to the state had not been resolved.

Norah Mlondobozi of the Mopani Farmers' Association (MFA), representing small-scale farmers, said: 'we have been through the workshops on security of land tenure where we know that the chiefs are not the owners, they are just custodians. So in the meetings we tell them, we know you are just custodians. So they don't have that power to threaten you to evict you.'[76]

This evidence suggests both the contested nature of local discussions of tenure and the possibilities for small landholders to challenge chiefs' claims of 'ownership' both in terms of customary law and also in terms of the Constitution. However, much depends on the local context and whether landholders have NGOs or other organisations to support them.

The scale of investment in land makes it difficult for chiefs to take it away. One of the most striking developments in the former homeland areas is the amount invested in modern houses using very largely the same kind of material as in the urban areas, such as concrete blocks and roof tiles. This is noted in the Integrated Development Plan for Mopani district (2016), which points out that many people prefer to retain their homes in the rural villages, and bring up children there, because they are seen as safer and culturally more appropriate. Land and related costs are lower and services such as electricity are now increasingly widespread.

Particularly in the areas near main roads, but even in deeper rural villages, there are signs of wealth: ten-roomed double-storeyed mansions with columned porticos and luxury vehicles parked in the driveway. Educated people with jobs in the public sector or those who have succeeded in the private sector feel that they have sufficient tenure security to build in such areas, whatever the legal situation. They may feel that their social position and political connections give them security, both because they have a capacity to defend themselves and because they have improved the land. Most of these houses are built without bonds and sometimes over a period of time when cash becomes available. Formal lenders do not generally see the land rights in these areas as sufficiently secure. Informal lending is possible through family or other networks.

However, some of the evidence from Khumisho Moguerane's essay on women house purchasers in the eastern

Free State borderlands suggests they have a slightly different perception. She demonstrates a very strong commitment by women to purchasing residential property in order to give themselves security and build a base for their families. Two of the purchasers had experienced the loss of allocated sites on communal land in which they had made some investment. Thus their preference, when they could afford it, was to purchase in a town or township in the Free State with private property. For them, the landholding regimes in the former homelands still presented too much uncertainty, although such families may try to retain plots there too.

In Limpopo, small roadside *chesa nyama* restaurants and car washes are also evident, and owners can get access to sites for this purpose at little cost, which also reduces startup and overhead costs.

Two further case studies illustrate the kind of arrangements being made to facilitate small-scale commercial farming. A male pensioner, originally an outsider, opened a shop and, as he put it, local people started to 'know him and like him'. He got to know the chief, who lent him her plot on the local irrigation scheme in exchange for maize meal. After a while she gave him a PTO for the plot, which he understood to denote ownership. An ageing friend gave him a nearby plot in the same irrigation scheme. They were both about 1 ha, and he gave one to his wife; they pay no rental or fee, and regard the land as theirs.

After the chief 'gave' him the land, he was freed from the obligation to supply her with maize and he planted tomatoes on most of it, enabling him to take up farming full-time. He also cultivates palms in pots for rental to wedding ceremonies and other functions. He supplies the Zion Christian Church with sugar cane for Good Friday. He has also benefitted from support from the Department of Agriculture, which gave him orange tree saplings and assistance with chemicals for two years.

He clearly feels sufficiently secure, even without title, to invest. Most of his efforts are on annual crops and movable pot plants, but the citrus does suggest a longer-term view. The ease of access and low cost of land gave him a start: his is an example of the benefits of informal or customary access. Purchasing a private, titled plot might have created insuperable barriers. The modified customary system, on the other hand, can be flexible.

By contrast, many people we interviewed had received or inherited agricultural plots for which they felt they had secure tenure, and were not farming these plots. The reasons given in this round of interviews were primarily about the lack of water. A woman in her late forties, working as a teacher in a township, but living in a village about twenty kilometres away, started cultivating vegetables in 2005 in her neighbour's backyard garden. She had a borehole on her own property, which she saw as essential. She has her own plot outside the village but does not cultivate it because it has no water supply. She approached the headman to ask if she could cut a different arable plot closer to the village but he refused. Instead she uses some open municipal land next to the road without any formal agreement and she does not pay rent.

The key point for her is to be near water to grow spinach and other vegetables. She has no tenure security; her neighbours and the municipality could change their minds at any time. But the vegetables she grows do not require long-term investment. Having land near home enables her to water and tend crops more easily. As a school teacher she has income to invest and can pay another woman to tend the gardens during the day. She grows vegetables to a high standard and sells to Food Lovers Market and Spar in Tzaneen.

Other interviewees mentioned lack of water as the single most important constraint on farming. However, lack of tenure security can be a constraint on investment in water supplies and Norah Mlondobozi of the MFA mentioned lack of access to credit in general as a factor inhibiting agriculture.

This detailed material from Limpopo speaks to the debate on tenure, although it does not provide any definitive answers. Allocation through customary/PTO grants clearly continues to play a vital role in giving poor people and newcomers access to land, including land that can be used for smallholder agriculture.

Registration should not restrict this access – which is largely on the former pasture lands around villages. Generally people feel secure on their allocated land, but it is difficult to expand holdings if they are not the direct users. A form of registered ownership would make this possible.

Investment in agricultural land is also constrained except in the case of irrigation schemes. Titling may not necessarily be the only answer to raising capital for agriculture.[77] For example, the Spar retail chain recognises that one of the greatest difficulties that small-scale farmers face when marketing their produce is that the crops do not meet the high standard required by most retailers. The Spar Rural Hub provides smallholders with necessary farm inputs, and also provides access to retail markets, through which input costs can be recuperated over time from a dedicated account held by the retailer to pay for produce. Nevertheless, credit remains a barrier and is largely now dependent on NGOs, retailers and alternative income.

RESTITUTION[78]

AFTER THE ANC-LED GOVERNMENT took office in 1994, land restitution was quickly put into operation by the Restitution of Land Rights Act 22 of 1994. This was planned as a limited process to redress land dispossession which had occurred through racially discriminatory legislation and practices during the era of segregation and apartheid, from the passing of the Natives Land Act in 1913 to its abolition in 1991. Claims had to be submitted to the Land Claims Commission by the end of 1998. However, the aims of restitution have been confused with broader aims of land redistribution and the scope of restitution has also expanded. Moreover, in 2014 a supplementary Restitution of Land Rights Amendment Act was passed that reopened the possibility for claims. In 2016, the Act was invalidated by the Constitutional Court but not before over 160,000 additional claims had been lodged, some of which were even more broad-ranging than those submitted initially.

Issues of restitution and tenure are closely linked. Restitution has largely taken place through CPAs, and we have discussed the uncertainty of family land rights in these collective landholding vehicles. The process of restitution was initially aimed at families and dispossessed communities. But chiefs and traditional authorities have played an increasingly significant role in the context of a general reassertion of their authority over land and local administration. In these aspects, as in policy more generally, the role of chiefs in the future of landholding is a central issue.

10

Historical misconceptions
Chiefs and the land

WE HAVE DISCUSSED BRIEFLY the history of land tenure, but want to return to the question of chieftaincy and land at this point because it has become so important in some recent restitution cases. Although chiefs are sometimes seen in old literature as controllers or even owners of land, this view is not justified by historical and legal material.

The relationship between chief and subject/citizen was based on political loyalty, and this gave rights to land and rights in land. Chiefs did not own land. In some areas of South Africa, depending on the period, people lived outside centralised kingdoms.[79] In pre-colonial times land was relatively abundant and this placed checks on the power of chiefs.[80] The role of chiefs and their councils was largely administrative in the allocation of land. Once it was allocated to homesteads, the families had strong rights in the land and it could generally be inherited by the family. New chiefdoms were in the main established over pre-existing populations who were already in possession of the land and who were often seen as having a special spiritual bond with it.

Most individuals received land not directly from the chief but through inheritance and local allocation by groups formed around a core of kin.[81] Land could normally only be taken away from households in the case of individuals being found guilty of witchcraft or as punishment for revolt against the chief. The family had exclusive possession of residential and arable land.

In Mpondoland, 'a woman had exclusive right to cultivate any area which she had once turned over, no matter how long it was kept lying fallow'. This prescriptive right to cultivate certain areas was inherited.[82] Communal pasture land formed the bulk of the areas of most chiefdoms and was open to all who had land allocations, subject to local practices around the control of grazing.

As we noted, A.J. Kerr, author of the only extended analysis of customary laws of property, considers the word ownership appropriate to describe these rights, although they did not exactly involve the same concept of ownership as in European common law. It was a right that was 'good against the world'. This is an important baseline from which to understand customary rights and it has in certain respects been recognised by the Constitutional Court.

However, this understanding is to some degree being challenged by an increasing reassertion of chieftaincy in South Africa and by restitution claims that place chieftaincy at their heart. In certain respects, the reassertion of chieftaincy is a legacy of apartheid.

The Bantu Authorities Act of 1951 was the foundation of the Bantustan or homeland policy and aimed to entrench conservative, traditional authority as the basis for political power and the administrative system in these areas. It provoked widespread resistance, with outright revolt in

Sekhukhuneland, Mpondoland and elsewhere. But by the end of the 1960s the system had been entrenched.

The process of establishing tribal authorities also led to a formal definition and demarcation of tribal territories. With the strong support of the state, many chiefs were able to rebuild power and assert control over local administration and land allocation.

The transition to democracy in 1994 and the final Constitution of 1996 did not envisage a major role for chiefs, but they have been in a good position to develop their authority in some rural areas. Government has gradually accepted a significant role for traditional authorities in rural administration and formalised their position in the Houses of Traditional Leaders and also in the 2003 Traditional Leadership and Governance Framework Act. President Zuma has seen the chiefs as valuable political allies. When the Restitution of Land Rights Amendment Act was passed in 2014, he explicitly encouraged chiefs to lead restitution claims. This process was already well under way, as we describe below.

Our discussion tries to map out an alternative path for restitution. The policy was not intended to recreate the old chieftaincies of pre-colonial South Africa, which had themselves grown and ebbed over a long period. It was fully realised that such a policy would be ethnically divisive and could be the basis for ethnic or tribal politics. The 1913 cut-off date was introduced partly because the ANC recognised that earlier claims were likely to be 'tribal' in nature, and would probably involve overlapping, conflicting and uncertain claims.[83] Even so, post-1913 claims were often complicated and sometimes overlapping too.[84]

11

Historical misconceptions

Community

IN THE 1970S AND 1980S the term 'community' became increasingly important in the lexicon of groups and individuals at the forefront of resistance to apartheid, forced removals, resettlement by the state, and coercive control by chiefs.[85] 'The community' was seen as an inherently progressive grouping imbued to some degree with a collective, democratic and even socialist ethos. It was believed that if communities could be freed from colonial manipulation, infiltration and corruption, they could become the building blocks of a new order.

Local communities of various kinds did play an important part in mobilising and sustaining resistance and in framing alternative organisational forms. They were, however, put under much greater strain by the transition to democracy and the corrosive impact of competition to secure and control resources, which could and did inflame internal divisions. These experiences revealed that strategies which imagined that individual household interests could readily be accommodated in wider community structures were unrealistic. Delius sounded a warning note in 1996: 'there is ... the danger that the currently pervasive rhetoric of "community" can shroud the countryside in a dense conceptual fog. The diverse and shifting cleavages, conflicts and identities within local level society ... provide ample warning against the expectation that organic communities lie latent in villages, waiting like Sleeping Beauty for development's kiss. And established networks of patronage and power are often able to monopolize or block new resources, whatever their intended destination.'[86]

Nevertheless, ideas about cohesive, democratic communities played an important part in shaping the policy and practice of restitution in which the claimants and recipients of land in the rural areas were usually a collectivity. This did not always apply in the urban areas.

There was broad consensus that the beneficiaries of land reform should be communities. This was evident in the CPA legislation of 1996 as the main vehicle through which land would be transferred to new recipients. As noted, the Act provided for private ownership of restituted land by the CPAs but did not specify the rights of individual households within the collectivity.

A further historical misconception which has had a profound impact on policy implementation is the understanding of the process of dispossession. Cherryl Walker, a land activist who was Chief Land Claims Commissioner for KwaZulu-Natal from 1995 to 2000, writes of a 'master narrative of loss and restoration'.[87] According to this narrative, Africans once lived in coherent egalitarian communities which had held land in common beneficially from 'time immemorial' until whites arrived, sowed discord and stole the land by sword and by pen.[88] The dispossession of Africans is often imagined as a linear process or single event. Historical research suggests that dispossession took place over long periods and that, for example, African families were able to stay on white-owned farmland well after conquest. Their world was changing, but some had opportunities to survive as tenants and sharecroppers until the beginning of the apartheid era.

Especially in the 1950s and 1960s, many were subject to forced removals under racially discriminatory legislation, but their experiences were often very different, with some displaced to rural dense settlements or to homelands while others moved to cities. Although organised for political purposes into communities that claimed restitution, the individual families in these groupings were often dispersed and fragmented. We need to take into account this social reality in thinking about the issues of restitution and community.

12

Recent case studies of restitution

RESEARCH WAS CONDUCTED BY Delius and Hay between 2013 and 2016 on three sets of land claims for the regional Land Claims Commission (RLCC) and the Land Claims Court (LCC). They give a sense of the complexities that emerged and the challenges that lay in the path of resolving claims. The first of these cases involved the Sabi Sand Wildtuin, a privately owned area, made up of 21 farms, which incorporates a number of luxury lodges and wildlife reserves. Eight community claims and nine individual/family claims were lodged on farms in this area. The two largest claims were by the Jongilanga Tribal Authority, for 18 farms in the area, and the Mhlanganisweni community, for 21 farms in the area.

The second case, from 2014 to 2015, involves research on the Moletele land claim together with competing and overlapping claims in the same area. The Moletele claim was a chiefly led, tribal claim for 56 farms in the Maruleng area of Limpopo Province. Some of the farms claimed by the Moletele community are presently part of other traditional authority areas. The Mnisi Traditional Authority lodged a claim which overlapped with the Moletele claim on three farms. The Moraba community initially lodged a separate claim for 15 farms (some of which overlapped with the Moletele claim) but this claim was combined with the Moletele claim in 2004.

Piet Mogane lodged a claim apparently over the entire former Pilgrim's Rest district (it was difficult to determine the exact extent, as the claim form is missing). The Sibaya/Sibuyi/Xivuri clan lodged a claim for two farms, which overlapped with the Moletele claim. This claim was later extended to include more farms. A number of small family claims were lodged on some of the farms claimed by the Moletele.

Thirdly, research was conducted in 2016 on a set of overlapping and conflicting claims over roughly 64 farms in the Phalaborwa area. Four BaPhalaborwa communities lodged separate tribal claims over farms surrounding their present locations, as well as joint claims over a portion of the Kruger Park.

The VaMakhuva community lodged a tribal claim which initially appeared to be over a portion of the Kruger Park, but was later said to extend over a very large area which overlapped with the farms claimed by the different BaPhalaborwa groups. The Balepye-Maenetja community was made up of two groups, which had initially lodged separate claims, but these were later combined. The claims over many of these farms were opposed by the Majeje Tribal Authority.

Most of the large claims were based on the loss of customary land rights. But the claims were presented not just as claims to ancestral land, but claims to former ancient tribal kingdoms. Furthermore, these ancient kingdoms were portrayed as ethnically exclusive or, at least, involved a dominant ethnically defined group that believed itself to have the authentic authority over the relevant area, with others subordinate to them.

For example, according to the Moletele claim: 'The whole area now inhabited by Setlhare Tribe, Nxumalo, Jongilanga, Mnisi Tribes [all Shangaan/Tsonga] belonged to the Chiloane and the other MaPulana Chiefs and their tribes regarded Chief Chiloane their paramount Chief and recognised and accepted him as such. Paramount Chiloane's paramountcy was crashed [sic] by the apartheid regime and in particular Native Affairs Commissioner "Bokweni".'

The basis of each of the BaPhalaborwa claims was that:

> The Community occupied the land from time immemorial and enjoyed ownership until they were finally removed in 1920's [sic] by the Assistant Native Commissioner Lydsdorp [sic] ... The Ba-Phalaborwa [Ba-Maseke–Selwane–Mashishimale–Makhushane] had customary unregistered rights over the land that they occupied. The land was on behalf of the Community kept in custody of the Chief ... When Act 27 of 1913 became law on the 19th of June 1913, the Ba-Phalaborwa people were the only people in occupation of the whole area between the Letaba and Olifants Rivers that they are now claiming back.

The VaMakhuva also claimed to have been the first people in occupation of the area between the Letaba and Olifants rivers, and that they were the ones who allowed the Sotho to live in the area; so the Sotho households in fact owed allegiance to them.

The Mhlanganisweni claimant community was different in that it was not a tribal claim based around a chieftaincy. It was widely known that the Mhlanganisweni community had been recently formed, specifically for the purpose of lodging a large land claim on behalf of some (not all) families who had originally come from the area. All claims involved the inclusion of people who had lived on and been evicted from farms in the surrounding areas. Furthermore, some of the individuals or families who had lodged separate claims over some of these same farms had been pressured to join these large claims and abandon their individual or family claims.

The main finding of Delius and Hay's historical research was that the tribal and community claims were either grossly inflated or lacked any support whatsoever. The VaMakhuva, BaPhalaborwa and Moletele chieftaincies, for example, were very small and weak, which partly guided the decision by the colonial government not to provide the Moletele with a location, and this also explains why the BaPhalaborwa and VaMakhuva locations were so small.

While there was evidence to support their claims to a small number of farms, in general it was clear that they did not have as much authority over the area as they claimed. Importantly, the idea that all Africans lived in tribes ruled by chiefs that 'owned' land on behalf of communities was deeply problematic and rooted in segregationist and apartheid ideology. In the area claimed by the Moletele for example, Delius and others found:

> There is no evidence of overarching political control over these farms exercised by the Moletele or any other chiefdom. There were significant clusters of followers of particular chiefs on some farms as shown in the discussion of individual farms. But even on these farms there were also residents with other or no political allegiances. The picture that emerges from our research

is of diverse interpenetrated groups with multiple forms of political allegiance living in the region. There were also high levels of mobility between and from the farms. The idea of exclusive tribal communities with effective control – especially in relation to land allocation – spanning some or all of these farms is not supported by the evidence. The increasing centrality of labour tenancy agreements also meant that farmers increasingly determined the nature and form of access to land.[89]

The findings in the BaPhalaborwa area were similar, except that there was far less settlement in the area in general, and no evidence to support any claim – not even a tenancy claim – to many of the farms. In the Sabi Sands area there was not only relatively sparse settlement, but there was no overarching political authority that controlled either land or the people living in the area.[90] Nevertheless, many families, some involved in the large claims, had clearly lost rights to land and deserved to be compensated.

Delius and Hay's Phalaborwa report was only really required for some of the farms under claim, because in fact the state had already purchased and transferred a number of farms to the Moletele, BaPhalaborwa and Balepye-Maenetja communities. This was done despite the complete lack of evidence to support some of the claims, and despite the existence of competing claims. In one startling case the state had purchased a farm and transferred it to a community that had in fact years earlier 'relinquished' its claim because, according to their lawyer:

When we determined the extent of the claim in 1998, we mistakenly assumed that the relevant western boundary of the —— land was the 1850 boundary. The truth, however, is that since 1850, the western border of —— had contracted considerably towards the east ... As the tribes can only reclaim the land rights that they lost after the 19th of June 1913, they realise that they must now relinquish their claims to farms that lie west of their 1913 border.

Other claims were included in the *Government Gazette* despite being relinquished years before. Not only did this reveal how poorly implemented, chaotic, and disconnected from history land restitution had become, but it was apparent that certain claims were being privileged over others. Worryingly, there seemed to be a tendency to support Sotho claims over Shangaan/Tsonga claims, based on the idea that the Sotho were the 'original' inhabitants of the region while Tsonga people only moved there later.

Smaller group claims were also amalgamated to form larger claims. For example, the Balepye and Maenetja groups were combined on the basis that they were in fact part of the same community. The Moraba claim was incorporated into the Moletele claim, despite both claims being based on the argument that the land under claim constituted different kingdoms, the one called Ga-Moraba, and the other being the Mapulana kingdom.

13

Implementation of land restitution

LAND RESTITUTION WAS NOT PLANNED with this level of complexity in mind. It was initially intended to be confined largely to a relatively small number of families and communities who had been forcibly removed under apartheid laws. This included especially removals under the Group Areas Act in the cities and the removal of African settlements that were unfortunately called 'black spots'. These were communities who held land, both in private and PTO or customary tenure, outside the boundaries of the Bantustans, and therefore within districts that were designed to be exclusively for white-owned farms. Apartheid policy aimed to segregate what had been, in some parts of the country, a chequerboard of white-owned and black-occupied land. Some of these groups had been at the forefront of rural political struggle in the apartheid era to prevent their forced removal and to oppose the apartheid system as a whole. They were the base for effective civic and residents' associations that increasingly identified with the United Democratic Front and the ANC. Resolving these land issues was therefore an urgent political task for the new government.

In 1995 the Minister for Land Affairs, Derek Hanekom, went so far as to say that 'the bulk of the cases which will be dealt with by the Commission of [sic] the Land Claims Court will be post-1948 cases', which is when the apartheid government came to power. He stressed once again that restitution was to deal with 'certain kinds' of dispossession only.[91] This view is part of what led initially to the setting of unrealistic deadlines by which land restitution was to be concluded. It also meant that the Land Claims Commission offices were small and under-equipped, and staff numbers were limited. Walker, as the first Land Claims Commissioner for KwaZulu-Natal, has revealed the huge institutional challenges faced by the RLCCs.[92]

When land restitution first began, three main agencies, the Commission for the Restitution of Land Rights, the Department of Land Affairs and the Land Claims Court were responsible for settling land claims.

The commission was meant to be a temporary entity which would operate for five years, during which time it was imagined restitution would be completed. The original support staff were primarily ad hoc employees on short-term contracts.[93] Initially it was assumed that the Department of Land Affairs, with its more permanent staff, would do the research and settlement of claims, and so RLCC offices were given 'a total complement of just six relatively junior administrative posts ... no provision was made for research, legal support and community facilitation, nor for trained registry staff to handle the rapidly mounting piles of paper.'[94]

In 1997 the commission identified numerous, basic administrative challenges that it needed to overcome. Even then it did not recognise the importance of establishing effective archiving or record-keeping systems. Until the other problems were resolved, the report stated, 'the Commission will continue to waste time, energy and resources trying to make a defective system work'.[95]

Some argued then (and have argued since) that the policy of land restitution had not been adequately advertised to rural people.[96] One group of activists in Limpopo, who established the Nkuzi Development Association, was proactive in ensuring that the opportunity for land restitution did not pass local communities by. They visited rural communities to assist in lodging claims, but, as Mark Wegerif, an activist and founder of Nkuzi, explained, this often meant going through chiefs, who were the de facto authorities of the area at the time.[97] It would have been difficult to reach rural people without going through those channels. They recognised that there were problems with this and they also assisted differently constituted communities and hoped that more democratic structures could be established within all claimant communities. This nevertheless helped to normalise a situation whereby chiefs were able to claim enormous areas of land from which they said their 'tribes' had been dispossessed, and other leaders were encouraged to lodge large claims.

The process was significantly different in other parts of the country. In the Eastern Cape, for example, NGOs such as the Border Rural Committee and the Transkei Land Service Organisation (TRALSO) alerted communities to the Act and assisted with early claims that did not involve traditional authorities. These groupings were critical of the role that chiefs had played in the homelands and keen to establish alternative local democratic structures. Simultaneously, they pursued opportunities for redistribution under the government's pilot land redistribution programmes. For example, activists such as Ezra Sigwela helped communities within Bizana district,

Transkei, submit claims as early as 1995 for areas from which they had been forcibly removed by the Transkei homeland government. These claimant communities were keen to keep traditional authorities at the margins throughout the next twenty years, and the cases (Hlolweni and Mgungundhlovu mentioned above) proved to be significant more generally.

However, especially in the northern provinces and KwaZulu-Natal, some chiefs lodged claims very early in the process, without any encouragement.[98] Claimants included those who felt they had lost out in the apartheid era, when access to land and economic resources was dependent on being recognised as a chief. The government had meddled in rural politics by arbitrarily or instrumentally recognising or deposing chiefs. Collaborating chiefs were also allocated a disproportionate share of the land purchased by the state to consolidate the homelands. Land restitution was seen by some as an opportunity to establish chieftaincies more firmly or to expand political fiefdoms.

Politically astute, educated and often business-minded individuals with rural roots also saw opportunities in land restitution. Deborah James has termed them 'brokers' as they played a critical role in bringing complicated government policy to uneducated rural people, and mediating between them and government officials, landowners and development consultants.[99]

For thousands of poor rural families who at one time or another had been evicted from a farm, land restitution seemed to offer both the possibility of redress and economic opportunity. But few had the knowledge to see how their specific experiences might fit in with the requirements of the Act. Land restitution brokers could try to play that role.

Some combined their pastoral role with personal ambition.

The communities they had access to – for example, people living in the same communal area, or those who were connected through a church network or were old acquaintances – had very often come to their present home from many different points of origin. The history of dispossession in Limpopo, for example, entailed the eviction of many households from many white-owned farms, in many separate incidents. Intermediaries, sometimes with the encouragement and support of NGOs and officials, tended to combine a number of individuals and communities into large and ambitious claims.[100]

And of course, many families and smaller groups also lodged claims, based on specific experiences of forceful eviction, when families were given a few days' notice to leave, were often chased from their houses at gunpoint, lost livestock or heavy household items like stone grinders and pots they couldn't carry, and watched as their houses were set alight.

As the implications of the policy began to dawn on white landowners and some lawyers, they saw the opportunity to get rid of unwanted farmland, make some money, or play a role in helping local black communities receive land after a century of having it taken away. At least a few farmers and lawyers encouraged, rather than simply responded to, land claims.

At first, the claims came in slowly, but these developments led to a flood – many of them large and quite problematic in relation to the Act. As noted above, the offices of the Land Claims Commission were ill-equipped to deal with them. The result was mounting chaos. Vital information – such as original claim forms, historical validity reports conducted in the early days of land restitution, lists of claimant beneficiaries, transcripts of oral interviews, correspondence, archival files requested from the National Archives – was frequently lost.

Inadequate systems meant that opportunities for the destruction of documents abounded – sometimes as the result of corrupt deals. Overlapping and competing claims to farms were not identified immediately, which has had particularly damaging consequences, with some claims emerging only after the land in question has been transferred to other claimants. Another outcome of these inadequate systems is that administrative and judicial settlements have been impeded and even precluded because the relevant documentation was, and often still is, unavailable.

Faced with approximately 80,000 claims by the cut-off date at the end of 1998, the commissions began to process them. In theory each claim would be researched to see if it was credible before it was rejected or gazetted.

The programme got off to a slow start when the Land Claims Commission tried to conduct thorough research on claims in order to reach just settlements. The complexity of the problem they confronted emerged starkly, with multiple overlapping and conflicting claims being but one example of how complicated the processes of loss and transformation had been in reality, and how difficult it was to establish with precision who the rightful beneficiaries actually were.[101] Some claims clearly exceeded the terms of the Act, brushing aside the cut-off date of 1913.

The consequence was a slow process of gazetting claims, and even less success in reaching final settlements. To give one example, approximately 15,000 claims had been lodged in KwaZulu Natal, but by April 2000 only 1,064 had been gazetted for further investigation, and only 13 claims had been settled. The then Regional Land Claims Commissioner, Cherryl Walker, recalls that when she stepped down, 'thousands of unprocessed claims lay buried in mute, brown-foldered mounds on desks and registry office shelves throughout the Commission offices'.[102]

From around 2000, increased pressure was brought to bear on the Land Claims Commission to deliver more rapid results. But this pressure from above was not accompanied by constructive suggestions and additional resources to assist in overcoming the difficulties. The limited research capacity that existed was further diminished by the departure of experienced officials who at least had a good grasp of how departmental, provincial and national archival systems could be utilised.

Probably the most critical skills required for land restitution research are a good grasp of the relevant legislation, the specific information required to validate or disqualify a claim, an understanding of how and where the information can be found in archives, and some experience of conducting oral history interviews.

Once evidence is gathered, it also needs to be critically assessed, which requires an understanding of the methodological challenges of different types of evidence. The level required for legal and historical research skills was ideally a doctoral or at least a master's degree. As the complexity of the issues became more evident, it would have been helpful if at this stage mentors with advanced research skills and long experience had been appointed to show how to unravel the most intractable cases.

This did not happen and most commission appointees did not have the required skills. There was an enduring but mistaken assumption that historical research was easy and that archives are straightforward.[103] The archives, especially local records, are partial and the material that survives was, of course, not written with a future land restitution process in mind.

Greater reliance was placed on oral information, but while oral material can be immensely valuable, it is also a particularly challenging form of evidence. While all sources are vulnerable to manipulation to fit a story, oral history is vulnerable to manipulation in the very process of its creation. Oral material is difficult and time-consuming to collect and interpret, and it often requires multiple informants to build a picture of historical land rights. Memories are partial and people are consciously or unconsciously influenced by recent political changes. Similarly, burial sites and memories of other physical features proved to be unstable sources of information.

In order to accelerate the process, claims were increasingly gazetted on the basis of a limited grasp of the law and superficial research. The historical narratives that were constructed and the legal justification of claims became increasingly uniform. It is clear that a basic template was used, applied with little concern for the particularities, strengths and weaknesses of each claim and unlikely to stand up to critical scrutiny or challenge. Research was increasingly delegated to consultants who used similar research methodologies and faced similar time constraints.

For example, in 2001 the activist group Nkuzi was given a contract to validate 2,140 land claims. Although they hired an extra eleven people to help with this project, each person would have needed to complete a report every three days (based on there being 250 workdays in a year). Even though they were strongly motivated, this clearly did not allow time for careful research.[104]

In the meantime, landowners tended to turn to conservative ethnologists who had previously supported the system of tribal authorities (and who frequently focused primarily on establishing whether a group constituted a 'tribe' and whether the claimant community was in fact the official, rightful branch of a chiefdom). The research conducted by these groups was often unhelpful; a fact that officials in the Land Claims Commission told us on more than one occasion.

One of the major bottlenecks in land restitution up to that point had been the necessity for all settlements to be sanctioned by the Land Claims Court. This created delays. To speed up the process, the Land Claims Commission was given the ability to settle claims administratively, out of court. All that this required, ultimately, was parties who were willing to negotiate. There were a significant number of marginal and insecure farmers who were willing sellers whether or not the claim on their land was well grounded in law or evidence. Some farmers who may have doubted the validity of a land claim did not have the motivation or the money to dispute it.

Gazetting did not in fact represent approval of a claim, but once land was gazetted it was difficult to raise credit and farmers were legally prohibited from making significant alterations to their land. Farmers did not wish to invest, even in necessary upkeep and improvements.[105] Some farmers, of course, did dispute claims, and those cases continued to clog the system.

Another strategy of the Commission, and sometimes claimants themselves, was to merge family claims and community claims into large overarching claims.[106] In the process, individual or family claims were often neglected, traditional leaders were privileged, and in some cases entirely new 'communities' were created on the basis of the merged claim – even if they had little in the way of shared histories, rules of land allocation, or experience of dispossession. Individual and family claims were already being discouraged, and this new development was justified as leading to the restitution of major resources. The commission then only had to deal with one claimant group rather than several, and to create one CPA. They were also spared the task of adjudicating between conflicting claims, something that would have required intensive historical research.

These strategies appeared to pay off. In the period after 2000 there was a significant increase in the number of claims officially settled. There is a great deal of scepticism about the reliability of the Department of Land Affairs' figures, and in fact the vast majority of settled claims were for relatively well-documented urban land and involved cash compensation, but there is no doubt that significant strides had been taken by 2007, with the Land Claims Commission declaring the finalisation of many large rural claims, and a significant amount of farmland being transferred to claimant communities. Or so it seemed.

If research had been done systematically and professionally prior to the gazetting of claims, and the commission had carefully read and interpreted the legislation, then speedy administrative settlement might have had its desired effects. Instead, an inadequate grasp of the implications of legislation has had dire consequences as court judgments have since thrown a spanner in the works of the commission.[107] Many of the settlements reached through negotiation came under scrutiny as new, conflicting and overlapping claims emerged years later thanks to the poor filing systems of the commission. Artificially created CPAs and trusts have experienced severe difficulties. And the administrative process of settling claims has made it possible for some dubious settlements to be reached. We will address each of these issues in turn.

The Land Claims Court clarified the issue of what constituted a 'community' in a number of judgments, such as *Kranspoort*, which were confirmed by higher courts.[108] The issue was revisited in the Constitutional Court in the *Goedgelegen* judgment handed down by Justice Moseneke in June 2007, which pointed out: 'our task is made slightly easier by the fact that the key term "community" has been defined in the land restitution legislation: Section 25(7) of the Constitution and section 2(1)(d) of the Restitution Act entitles a community dispossessed of a right in land after 19 June 1913 to claim restitution or other equitable redress: "A community, unless the context otherwise indicates, is any group of persons whose rights in land are derived from shared rules determining access to land held in common by such group."'[109]

The judgment reiterated that shared rules, and not the presence or absence of some form of traditional authority, was the crux of the matter. The judge found that the Land Claims Court in this instance was wrong to hold that the applicants were not a community because they did not have an accepted tribal identity, or that they did not live under the authority of a chief designated by tribal hierarchy, or that they did not occupy the land in accordance with ancient customs and traditions. None of these attributes are requirements in themselves or collectively. This ruling should have diminished any perceived pressure to merge community claims with those of traditional leaders. But it did not have that effect in practice and it appears that the commission has ignored both the *Goedgelegen* and *Kranspoort* judgments.

Nevertheless, the reassertion of the definition of a community made it clear that the large numbers of artificially constructed groupings would not survive scrutiny in a court of law. This was particularly plain in relation to the community claims put forward by labour tenant families, which had been encouraged by officials, activists and brokers at various stages of the process. An earlier ruling by Justice Dodson affirmed that there must be 'a sufficiently cohesive group of persons' to show that 'there is a community or a part of a community, regard being had to the nature and likely impact of the original dispossession on the group; and ... some element of commonality between the claiming community and the community as it was at the point of dispossession'. This placed large claims by recently constituted community groups in legal jeopardy.[110]

The *Goedgelegen* judgment also had another major consequence. It ruled that labour tenants did not have to have been removed through direct state action or as a result of a specific piece of legislation to have suffered dispossession on a racially discriminatory basis. Eviction by white farmers in a context of generalised racial discrimination was sufficient ground for claims by individual labour tenants. This ruling therefore offered to support vast numbers of claims by individual labour tenants while closing the door on most of the community claims into which they had been amalgamated.

Once again, the land commissions do not seem to have fully comprehended the implications of the judgment. The reopening of the process in 2014 seems to have created further confusion on this front. Lawyers and agents have apparently resubmitted labour tenant claims, which had been merged into communities, as individual claims again. The process is now in limbo, but at some point the commission may have to confront the complex task of sorting out duplicated claims.

Another very time-consuming process, which to an outsider at least appears to be at odds with the Dodson and Moseneke judgments, has been the policy and practice of assuming that the beneficiaries include all the living claimants and all of the descendants of now-deceased claimants. This is an enormous research exercise especially in relation to large amalgamated claims and to claims which relate to the more distant past. It takes a significant amount of time and resources to complete. It is also doubtful whether all of the people who might be eligible within the very wide definition have been included. This strategy does not operate on the basis of a 'community' that exists in the present. It also creates vast lists of potential beneficiaries dispersed over wide areas, which both dilutes the value of settlements for each claimant and makes it even less likely that effective representative structures can be created. It furthermore creates the potential for a large number of people to get rights in a CPA over time, diluting any income they receive and creating difficult conditions for decision making.

The alternative is to operate on the basis of a more narrowly defined past community with 'shared rules in access to land' and a contemporary community which is 'sufficiently cohesive' and with 'some element of commonality between the claiming community and the community as it was at the point of dispossession'. This approach, following the judgments mentioned, may create disputes about who should and who shouldn't be included. But it provides the basis for more effective land restitution and the management of land.

The settlement of claims has proceeded more quickly in recent years in some provinces, such as the Eastern Cape. Court proceedings have sometimes resulted in negotiations in which the lawyers concerned, rather than the commission itself, have negotiated compromises, such as at Camperdown in KwaZulu-Natal, where those owners who wish to withdraw from farming have agreed to transfer and the beneficiaries accepted the land or payment.

In 2014, lawyers arrived at a settlement of the Wild Coast Sun claim (Mgungundhlovu) after nineteen years of disagreement and uncertainty. There has been a tendency to arrange large negotiated settlements in KwaZulu-Natal where claims often involved chiefs. These have also increased the amount of land being transferred, a high priority for the commission and the department, which need to show evidence of some land transfer. However, CPAs and trusts, which are the instruments through which communities hold land after restitution settlements, have experienced difficulties.

Despite the efforts of the commission, overlapping and conflicting claims have simply not gone away. These claims have had to go before the Land Claims Court, which has in some cases found that the commission's research prior to and after gazetting was too weak to proceed with the case. The Department of Rural Development and Land Reform was instructed to provide more credible research, which it was often not able to do. Court cases were delayed by the necessity to commission new research, clarify the position of all claimants, and interview stakeholders. Large, overlapping claims, which have been amalgamated, are among the most difficult to resolve requiring long research processes.

Once old-order claims are settled, new-order claims will need to be settled. Before the Restitution of Land Rights Amendment Act of 2014 was set aside, up to 160,000 new claims had already been lodged, and it was estimated by the Regulatory Impact Assessment that 397,000 new claims are likely to be lodged with the CRLR.[112] At its present rate of finalising 560 claims a year, new-order claims that have already been lodged will take 143 years to settle, and if land claims are reopened and the expected 397,000 are lodged, it will take 709 years to complete the process of land restitution.

Table 1: Projected rate of finalisation and settlement of claims *(according to 2015/16 performance and 2016/17 targets)*[111]

Claims to be finalised or settled as of 19 August 2013 (1)	Performance according to Annual Reports (2)			Remaining claims as of June 2016 (based on column 1-4):	Total claims to be settled or finalised as at March 2017 (3)	Years to be settled and finalised at 2015/16 rate of performance	Target for claims to be settled or finalised according to annual performance plan 2016/17 (4)	Years to be finalised at targeted rate according to annual performance plan
	2013/14	2014/15	2015/16					
Settled	8,733	270	428	617	7,418	7,419	12	615	12
Finalised	20,592	292	372	560	19,368	N/A	34.6	454	42.7

CPAs and trusts which were created through the consolidation of claims have often fractured.[113] Relationships with the commission have deteriorated. This causes even further delays, with meetings cancelled at the last minute, and factions within a CPA refusing to meet or negotiate with one another. On a number of occasions we have travelled for hours deep into rural areas with officials from the Land Claims Commission, only to find that the community we were meant to meet had decided to cancel without notice. When meetings do occur, officials and researchers sometimes face a hostile crowd which, understandably, is angry that settlements have been so long delayed. It is not surprising that the commission has a high turnover of staff, who must tire of spending their weeks and even weekends in such unrewarding pursuits.

Another outcome of administrative settlement and the bypassing of proper research was that the integrity of the restitution process was easily compromised. Farms have been given to communities that do not have valid claims on the land. The diversion of significant resources – both administrative and financial – that these incidents entail has further delayed the settlement of legitimate claims.

14

Mala Mala in Sabi Sands

An expensive illustration of some of the flaws in the system

THE MALA MALA EXAMPLE SHOWS the possibility for flagrant abuse of the system, allowing for the enrichment of elites rather than the empowerment of the poor. Initially, the owners of the farms that made up the Sabi Sand Game Reserve decided to collectively resist the claims on the land. But in 2007, without consulting the other owners, the Rattray family, which owned Mala Mala, decided to break ranks and accepted the validity of the Mhlanganisweni claim. While there were a number of claimants, the Mhlanganisweni group was particularly strongly supported by the commission and various legal representatives.

The Mhlanganisweni claim was gazetted as the overarching claim without a process of consolidation of claims being agreed on or formalised. The 'community' was quite obviously formed specifically for the purpose of lodging land claims over a large area – it had no historical basis or cohesion. But once the validity of the claim was accepted by the owners and the commission, the key issue in dispute became the value to be placed on the land, and whether or not it was reasonable for the state to purchase it.

While the commission initially agreed to a payment of R740 million, this was rejected by the minister and subsequently by the Land Claims Court. In 2012 Delius was asked to research the strength of the historical evidence for the wider range of claims in Sabi Sands. Mala Mala was included in the remit to ensure comprehensive coverage of all the overlapping claims.

The report by Delius and Hay showed that the claim to Mala Mala was among the least credible of all of those submitted. Nonetheless, the decision of the Land Claims Court was taken on appeal to the Constitutional Court. Shortly before the case was heard, the Presidency intervened, the case was withdrawn and Mala Mala reserve was bought by the state for over R1 billion.[114] This was the single most expensive farm purchase in the South African land restitution process.

Ownership was in part vested in a newly created 'Nwandlamhlari community', which was formed by merging the Mhlanganisweni claimants with overlapping and competing claimants. Some of the members of the new community had made no mention of the Mala Mala farms in their original claims.[115] Unsurprisingly there is growing evidence that this entirely fictitious community is racked by bitter internal disputes. The fact that approximately R300 million more was paid for Mala Mala than the highest valuation previously made, which was already deemed too high by the minister, also fuelled speculation that major corruption was involved. This suspicion deepened when it emerged that David Mabunda, previously Land Commissioner and then CEO of the National Parks Board, had been appointed as a director on the Mala Mala board in 2010. He acquired a significant shareholding, which was estimated in newspaper reports to be worth R81 million when Mala Mala was sold.[116]

15

CPAs, chiefs and ethnicity

IN THE CONTEXT OF LONG DELAYS and massive group claims, settlements have had disappointing results.[117] The commission has not always had the money to purchase farms quickly from farmers, and negotiation processes have been slow, with the result that farms become run down long before transfer actually takes place.

It is important to consider for a moment the situation in which landowners have found themselves when they have decided to accept a claim on their farm and reach a settlement with the commission. Contrary to popular belief, farmers are in some cases paid less than market value for their farms – we have even heard of farmers being threatened by the commission to accept lower valuations for their farm or face anger, and perhaps theft or violence, from communities for delaying the settlement of a claim.

Farmers selling their farms in this context often face difficult economic choices and – aside from the few who try to cheat the system into getting above-market pay-outs – find themselves in straitened financial circumstances. The longer a settlement takes to be reached, or a transaction to be finalised, the harder it is on the farmer's pocket. In this context, farms stop running effectively, workers are laid off, investment stops and basic maintenance is neglected so that by the time farms are finally acquired by the state, the land is much reduced in value and potential.

The main point here is that it is not generally 'unwilling' and 'uncooperative' farmers who cause delays in the process and who intentionally ruin good farms in order to sabotage the programme of land restitution. There are also of course cases where some farmers have intentionally been obstructive, misleading and even tricked the commission into making poor choices (such as failing to include packing sheds and important machinery in settlements), but these cases are not the prime cause of the widespread failure of land restitution projects.

When farms have been transferred to communities, difficulties relating to 'communal' ownership often emerge.[118] The failure of the vast majority of farm-based settlements, whether under traditional leadership or CPAs, is well known and accounts of corruption are legion. A widespread and largely accurate perception is that it is the leaders and not the ordinary members of these groupings who reap the rewards. In addition, many claimants, especially younger members of claimant groups, have little appetite for life on the land.

The process of forming CPAs has also had its share of difficulties in the Eastern Cape. The Hlolweni claim (North Pondoland Sugar) in former Transkei was successfully taken to court, and judgment given by Judge Bam of the Land Claims Court in favour of the claimants over 10,000 ha of land that had been confiscated by the Transkei Development Corporation for a sugar project. However, it took two years to form a CPA and the authority of this CPA is disputed by the local chief, who argues that CPAs cannot be formed on land controlled by chiefs and traditional councils within the former homelands. The Eastern Cape government and the commission have to some degree shared this view. In the meantime, plans to develop a very large area of valuable land are in limbo.

Given the poor outcomes of transferring land, an obvious question is why cash settlements have not been used more widely in relation to rural claims, particularly as cash settlements were critical in expediting urban claims. This question is given even greater salience by the fact that over the last five years or so of intensive work on claims, we have heard preference expressed by many ordinary claimants for cash settlements. Whether this would have been the case ten years ago, we cannot say. But for claimants who have waited since 1998 for their claims to be adjudicated, many of whom are old, in poor health, and living on social grants, cash has clear advantages over uncertain and slow-moving processes of land grants. To benefit effectively from land awards, families have to face disruptive moves.

Yet their voices have been drowned out or at least muted by leaders and officials who have strongly discouraged claimants from accepting cash settlements. There seems to be a number of factors at play. Leaders – especially the more affluent and entrepreneurial individuals who in practice drive these claims – are interested in securing control over significant resources rather than fragmented transfers to individual claimants. Officials are in part motivated by the ambitious targets the government has set for the redistribution of land to black South Africans, and the shifting but always urgent deadlines they have been given for this task. Once again, we can see the imperatives of land redistribution targets shaping the restitution programme, but ironically also contributing to its slow progress.

A common refrain from officials and leaders alike is that people won't be able to handle significant cash settlements and will squander the money. This is of course a deeply patronising view which deprives rural dwellers of choices available to their urban counterparts. It also contributes to the tragic reality that many of the individuals who lived through the trauma of eviction and removal and ended up dumped in poverty-stricken locations have died, or will die, without the comfort that cash compensation might have provided in their declining years. Bernadette Atuahene has shown that these assumptions about wasteful consumption in the case of cash payments are questionable, and that most beneficiaries use cash settlements to enhance both their own lives and the prospects of their families.[119]

Even as land restitution has been hamstrung by difficult cases, overlapping and conflicting claims, fractious communities, and even though settlements arrived at with difficulty have had poor outcomes, the government decided to reopen land claims in 2014. The main reason given for this was that many people who were eligible for land restitution had not been aware of the policy before the first deadline of 31 December 1998 to lodge claims. The reopening of land restitution placed a monumental burden on the Land Claims Commission, which now faced further overlapping claims, and the possibility that it would be found that some settlements had 'gone to the wrong people', as one official remarked.

This policy change was accompanied by rhetoric which encouraged chiefs to claim on behalf of people – and for people to go through chiefs to lodge claims. A well-publicised example was when President Jacob Zuma encouraged the

House of Traditional Leaders to get legal advice in lodging large claims 'on behalf of their people'.[120] But this sentiment has been widespread.[121] At the public hearing on the Land Restitution Amendment Bill of 2013 held in Sekhukhune district in November 2013, a parliamentarian admonished the audience for asking for title deeds, because they were not part of 'our culture ... I want to say to you people, yes, we want our land, but our chiefs, they must be our eyes, in our land'.[122] In Nelspruit, where members of the public complained about the uneven distribution of funds within trust committees, and suggested 'chiefs should make their own claims like other citizens and not launch their claims on behalf of their communities', 'people were urged to respect their chiefs, as they are the "custodians of culture"'.[123] At a parliamentary hearing on the Amendment Bill in February 2014, the Minister of Rural Development and Land Reform argued that concerns about land being returned to traditional leaders 'reflected "colonial" viewpoints'. He argued: 'Land had been removed from traditional leaders as custodians of the land, so their position could not be discounted.'[124]

The encouragement of tribal claims seems to cut directly across the earlier intentions of the first restitution Act and, as noted, threaten an ethnicisation of local landholding and politics. It seems to tie in with the more general direction of President Zuma's government to extend authority to chiefs and traditional councils.[125] The speed with which the Bill passed through Parliament, despite significant opposition and warnings from almost all stakeholders in land restitution – including land rights activists, claimant groups, agricultural unions and historians – raised further questions about the purpose of the Bill.

The reopening of land claims was also used by some

lawyers to change the nature of the claims of their clients in order to make them stronger – for example, separating out legitimate labour tenancy claims over single farms from problematic large community claims over many farms. The recent setting aside of the Land Restitution Amendment Act by the Constitutional Court has, sadly, not entirely resolved the difficulties created by the passing of the Act in the first place.

The additional claims have been lodged, and will need to be dealt with in some way. The court's judgment is that claims lodged between 1 July 2014 and 28 July 2016 must be held in abeyance while Parliament considers passing a new law within two years. But people's expectations have been raised and they will likely be angry and disappointed if they are not met.

This anger could further inflame ethnic tensions in Mpumalanga and Limpopo. Chiefly-led land claims over large areas rest on the assumption that some communities, based on their origin, have a deeper connection to particular areas of land than others. They see themselves as 'rightful owners' of the land to whom should accrue all economic benefits of the claims. In Mpumalanga for example, Tsonga people are considered by some to be 'immigrants' from Mozambique. In fact, many migrated into the area before the colonial boundaries were entrenched. In the large Phalaborwa versus Makuba land claim, Tsonga speakers were described as being 'imported on a large scale' to serve whites. Readers of the claimants' history, which, it must be emphasised, was based on testimony given by Kgoshi Brown Malatji in the context of homeland boundary disputes, would see that he used the word 'majeje', meaning 'grass cutting termite', for 'foreigners who came from Mozambique to eat up our land'.[126]

The wording of the report systematically dehumanises local Tsonga speakers, and the comparison with insects is a chilling echo of xenophobia elsewhere.

The Land Claims Commission seems to be legitimising the idea that land restitution is about returning land to 'indigenous' people, the 'original' settlers, rather than respecting the Restitution Act, which explicitly states that claimants should qualify on the basis of dispossession through racially discriminatory practices *after 1913*. The implications of the shift towards indigeneity are troubling.[127] The logical consequences of neglecting such clear provisions become even more alarming. In the Western Cape, Khoi nation claimant groups say that the Western Cape, or even the entire country, 'rightfully' belongs to them as the indigenous people. A leader of a Korana claimant group stated, 'The government call themselves African people, but they don't know the history of Africa. They are not African people. They are invaders – they are foreigners.'[128]

16

Popular perceptions of the reality of restitution and CPAs

A HIGH LEVEL PANEL was appointed by Parliament in 2016 in order to investigate legislation that might address poverty, unemployment, inequality and nation-building in the country. Under the chairmanship of former president Kgalema Motlanthe, land has been a central focus. Public hearings gave an opportunity for those who had received land across the country to express their views on the outcomes of restitution. Their frustration and anger were palpable and, while a range of problems were identified, what was most striking was the extent to which the government is blamed. We have quoted some excerpts to provide a sense of the comments. Full recordings of these meetings are available online.[129]

> *Because of the CPA Act, the communities are always in conflict, they fail to make productive decisions, and thus hampering the improvement of food security, reduction of poverty and the improvement of the livelihoods of the beneficiaries.* (Lefa Berrington Maboela, Limpopo Communal Property Institutions Forum, High Level

Panel public hearings: Limpopo province, morning session, 14 March 2017)

Land amounting to 1000s of hectares was restituted to over 65 ... families, and farming equipment, irrigation networks and other water sources such as boreholes, immovable properties such as houses and storage facilities were part of the total package of the land parcel given to the communities ... Today I stand here before you and all I can account for is an eye-sore of ruins ... I can account for stretches of land that lies unattended and unproductive, I can also account for 100s of poverty-stricken and under-developed beneficiaries of the failed restitution process. The million worth of the land is nonexistent in the minds of many beneficiaries like me ... (Mr K. Dingiswayo, North West)

We should ensure that the amendment bill on the CPAs (Communal Property Act) does not affect the power, the rights and privileges of the CPAs ... because the eroding of these powers would mean government has given back as promised but it has also taken back that which is supposed to be belonging to people. (Mr K. Dingiswayo, North West)

Our communities were never capacitated on what a CPA is, what role are they to play and so forth ... for centuries, there was a misconception that 'Magoshi ke beng mabu' the land belongs to the chiefs, then those chiefs must exert control on every piece of land and the households of those who occupy the land. (Billy Masha, High Level Panel public hearings: Limpopo province,

RESTITUTION

morning session, 14 March 2017)

> *... there were supposed to be elections, members refused to vacate their positions, and there were conflicts. We tried to show them the law and our constitution but they still refused to vacate their positions on the CPA ... there was no accountability, there were no reports produced and no financial records shown to the community.* (Billy Masha, High Level Panel public hearings: Limpopo province, morning session, 14 March 2017)

These quotes represent a small selection of dissatisfied voices around dysfunctional CPAs – a critical issue for restitution in particular because they have been the main vehicle through which claimants receive land. Some speakers noted the tendency of chiefs or other powerful local brokers to try to dominate CPAs and undermine the provisions that are intended to make CPAs democratic, inclusive and accountable bodies. Further dissatisfaction relates to anxieties that the government might take land away from unproductive and dysfunctional CPAs. Mr Dingiswayo, for example, explained that his community now stood to 'forfeit' the land they had been awarded, 'because it is termed unused land with economic value'.

In Limpopo, a spokesman described a 'second phase of dispossession'.

> *This will be the 2nd phase of dispossession of the only asset of which we could stand up and claim our value as humans in the face of the earth.*
>
> *We think that the government ... is led by vultures. Imagine a parliamentarian coming down to us, just to*

loot our money ... Since the land claims commission was not time framed, they developed an interest in our claims and they started to loot everything there. It's chaos indeed. (Mamatlepa Phetole from Kgashane Mamatlepa community, High Level Panel public hearings: Limpopo province, afternoon session, 14 March 2017)

You passed legislations that encouraged us to put up land claims, and when the claims that we put gets successful, the land end up belonging to corrupt civil servants. When they realize that a plot of claimed land has some minerals, they take that for themselves, and that pains us. We were even surprised that there is a budget for post settlement support ... since 2008 we have been engaged in this battle and are surprised to hear that this budget was used for other purposes whereas it should have been given to us. We don't receive any assistance from the state, and what is disgusting is that some of your ministers have taken our land ... Must we allow the government that we elected to treat us as outcasts? (Bakgatla ba Mocha, High Level Panel public hearings: Limpopo province, afternoon session, 14 March 2017)

The current government land restitution programmes are marred by corruption, where you find corrupt government fighting over small patches of land that is supposed to be handed over to communities. Some community members who lodged complaints are kept in the dark by government officials who fraudulently alter the names and numbers of people on the beneficiary lists. Some people who are supposed to be listed in court proceedings are deliberately and fraudulently left outside the process in order to dilute their claims or in order for corrupt government officials to personally benefit from the land claims. (Themba Mzimela, University of KwaZulu-Natal, High Level Panel: KwaZulu-Natal session 1, 20 October 2016)

How come, Mr Motlanthe, that your people who are working for government, who don't have farms, now suddenly have farms, it means they are using our farms. (Unidentified speaker, High Level Panel public hearings: Limpopo province, afternoon session, 14 March 2017)

These quotes represent the most common themes of evidence on the topic of land restitution heard in the public hearings. Speaker after speaker pointed out that claimants have seen little or no benefit from land restitution themselves, even though in some cases their claims had supposedly been finalised. They pointed to a lack of communication, but most of all they blamed corruption, articulated a deep distrust of government, and highlighted the murkiness of land restitution settlements. Speakers blamed these problems on a failure to stick to a timeframe and a lack of monitoring and supervision. They also stated that the government is too close to a landowning elite whom they protect – and join – at the expense of the poor.

Mamatlepa Phetole gave the example of ZZ2, one of South Africa's largest agri-businesses, owning substantial properties in Limpopo and other provinces:

ZZ2 company is the advisor to the premier when it comes to agriculture, it is also the advisor to the president when it comes to agriculture, and the land that we have claimed, among other farms is the land that ZZ2 is staying there. Do you think that ZZ2 can advise Zuma to take that land and give back to the communities? They will hold the land, so we are not very comfortable with this government. (Mamatlepa Phetole from Kgashane Mamatlepa community, High Level Panel public hearings: Limpopo province, afternoon session, 14 March 2017)

Another speaker said:

those people that we have elected in government are in the pockets of those who oversee the land ... Government must have a policy in place, to ensure that there is in-depth declaration of interests so that there will be full disclosure on the part of anybody who is elected into government/ parliament. They must declare their interest, especially if they have interests in land the communities have claimed. Some of these politicians have farms, and when you check, many of them are conflicted. Do you think that they will agree to a motion in Parliament that says let us take some farms and give to communities? They are conflicted. Many speakers mentioned the fact that many farms are converted into lodges, and they are owned by people who are overseas, some of our leaders have shares in those lodges hence their silence when issues concerning these lodges are raised. (Unnamed speaker, High Level Panel public hearings: Limpopo province, afternoon session, 14 March 2017)

A further key issue arising from the public hearings as well as our submission to the High Level Panel is that there is

RESTITUTION

too much overlap between the function of the Land Claims Commission to resolve claims in a neutral manner, and its other functions to negotiate what happens 'post-settlement'. As one speaker suggested: *For the commission on land claims to be efficient, it must be autonomous from the Department of Rural Development and Land Reform.* (Lefa Berrington Maboela, Limpopo Communal Property Institutions Forum, High Level Panel public hearings: Limpopo province, morning session, 14 March 2017)

Some statements blamed government directly, rather than others who might have a stake in policy:

As government … you are now exaggerating hatred between Blacks and Whites. We are now facing the Whites as our enemy, while our real enemy is the government. (Mamatlepa Phetole from Kgashane Mamatlepa community, High Level Panel public hearings: Limpopo province, afternoon session, 14 March 2017)

You are putting blame on traditional leaders, but it is you who have given these unaccounted-for powers. (Bakgatla ba Mocha, High Level Panel public hearings: Limpopo province, afternoon session, 14 March 2017)

As the people, we will fight with our traditional leaders, while in fact they don't have a problem, the problem lies with those we have elected into government. (Unnamed speaker, High Level Panel public hearings: Limpopo province, afternoon session, 14 March 2017)

In summary, the public hearings provide evidence of popular

perceptions of those involved as beneficiaries of restitution. Many speak of the deep divisions sown through land restitution, as a consequence of overlapping and competing claims and the dysfunctional CPAs. Some point to the opportunities that restitution has created for outsiders. Some speakers said that the government actively encourages people to blame other groups for problems the government in fact has caused. Specifically, speakers pointed out that the government was trying to exacerbate racial divisions between whites and blacks, when in fact government officials are themselves capturing the benefits of land restitution at the expense of claimants. There were mixed views on chiefs and traditional councils, some suggesting that they are unnecessarily blamed and others that government has given them 'unaccounted for powers'.

17

Recommendations for restitution

THE SCALE AND COMPLEXITY of the problems we have outlined are not amenable to simple or quick fixes. But we believe that steps can be taken in the short term which will facilitate credible completion of all the claims lodged by 1998 and prevent the duplication of the current difficulties in the next phase of resolving claims.[130]

The immediate focus should be on researching outstanding land claims, and for this purpose the Land Commission needs to be provided with more staff, resources and training or to employ experienced researchers who have worked with the courts and lawyers to resolve claims. Ideally, both should happen simultaneously so that new staff in the commission can be trained while research is progressing. Effective filing and archives are also important.

Unreasonable deadlines – such as the one to settle all outstanding land claims in the next 24 months – are unhelpful and should be extended or dropped. Research into settling claims is time-consuming and cannot be rushed. Targets should be linked to a realistic understanding of the scale of the task and the need for appropriate skills. Section 9 of the Restitution Act should be used to appoint an independent, qualified research panel to oversee research, read reports and ensure that they meet adequate standards.

This unit should:
- screen all claims, starting with those that have been referred to the Land Claims Court but are not progressing;
- consider objectively if claims meet the requirements under section 2 of the Act;
- if not, amend the commission's recommendation to the Land Claims Court in the referral report to dismissal of the claim, or if the claim has not yet been referred to court, de-gazette the claim in terms of section 11A and apply section 11(3) or (4);
- where the commission has improperly consolidated claims and the consolidated claim has been referred to the Land Claims Court, either the referral must be withdrawn or the referral report must be amended to provide for the referral of the distinct claims;
- where the commission has created an artificial, consolidated community, either the referral must be withdrawn or the referral report must be amended to remove any reference to the artificial community and substitute the true claimants as the claimants before court.

Although there is little possibility that the government will meet the requirements set out by the Constitutional Court for the validation of the Restitution Amendment Act by 2018, it is important that these arrangements are in place before the new claims lodged under that process are considered. There will be considerable political pressure to settle these claims, and the commission requires sufficient support and expertise to deal with them effectively and also to reject invalid claims – including extensive claims for chieftainship and past kingdoms.

The Land Claims Court has been operating for some years with temporary judges seconded to it. The court needs to be stabilised by the appointment of permanent Land Claims Court judges, including a Judge President, so that an effective body of expertise, experience and consistency can be built up.

The legal requirements for restitution need to be respected, particularly the cut-off date of 1913, and claimants need to have had ten years of beneficial occupation of specific land. This is particularly the case when deciding what to do with large tribal claims for former (often imaginary) kingdoms. These claims are divisive and are otherwise problematic in that they are based on a misperception of the role of chiefs in land tenure systems. They misconstrue the experience of some African societies in the pre-colonial and early colonial eras and conflate the idea of political territory with ownership of land by a chief. The commission and the land claims process should not be a vehicle which entrenches chieftaincy in South Africa.

As part of this process the commission needs to recognise that many community claims are not going to survive scrutiny by the courts. The nature of a claim is determined at the time that it is lodged by the person lodging it. It can't be changed. If it was lodged as an individual claim, it must be treated as such. And if lodged as a community claim, it must be assessed as a community claim, and if the alleged community does not comply with the definition of community, then this should form part of the assessment.[131]

Willingness to entertain cash settlements would greatly assist in settling claims speedily. This could also help to create more certainty for existing landholders. It would help to free up the countryside for the government's programmes of redistribution, which would involve assisting people who are primarily interested in farming.

Serious consideration should be given to making the final phase of the restitution process document-based. Oral evidence would still of course be admissible in the claim, and tested in the process of research and assessment. However, once the documentation of the evidence, oral and written, is complete, the court should ideally make its decision on what is before it. While there may be instances where further oral research is needed, especially when there are major conflicts of evidence, this is a time-consuming process. A clearer procedure would speed up the decision-making process of the Land Claims Court on claims.

The commission should be placed under the direct control of a strengthened Land Claims Court once the issue of the appointment of its judges has been resolved. Alternatively, liaison arrangements between the institutions should be improved, if necessary by legislation. Formal reporting should be enforced on progress in the implementation of the Restitution Act to Parliament and to the Judge President of the Land Claims Court at specified intervals, say yearly or every second year. This should involve a written report, as well as a process of accounting to the court in person.

Amendments to the CPA Act are also urgently required. These should include procedural provisions to allow decisive and effective intervention where CPAs and trusts have become dysfunctional, particularly as a result of consolidation of claims, creation of artificial communities or failure to apply the *Kranspoort* judgment. There should also be more effective provision for post-settlement support with the appointment of administrators or attorneys to assist CPAs in navigating the complex financial and legal requirements of owning and developing productive enterprises. The lack of post-settlement support is a major problem that should be addressed urgently if the outcomes of restitution are to be improved for the beneficiaries.

Some routes forward

WHILE THE GOVERNMENT IS COMMITTED to pursuing land reform, the political rhetoric around land has become more feverish. Our aim is to avoid racialised rhetoric and suggest some practical and workable solutions to complex problems. Our research suggests that security of tenure for off-register landholders is particularly neglected and should be addressed as an urgent priority. Solutions are unlikely to be achieved in the short term, but clear policy directions can be set that will increase certainty.

Similarly, we advocate a series of practical steps towards resolving the backlog in restitution and suggest strongly that this process should have both more effective and clearer procedures and clear boundaries. The original aims, which envisaged a limited and demarcated intervention, should be restored.

Our proposals take account of key social and economic processes in South Africa. We recognise that urbanisation continues at a rapid pace and should provide a context for rural and peri-urban policies. A racially fuelled fantasy that urbanisation could be restricted lay at the heart of the violence, as well as the ultimate failure, of the apartheid system. Our strategies are aimed both at facilitating urbanisation and at creating potential benefits for rural families.

Siyabu Manona, Rosalie Kingwill and others are protagonists of a fundamental intervention in the shape of a Land Records Act that would record and recognise all off-register land rights, in all their complexity, and provide an effective administrative and dispute resolution system for the future. It is an ambitious proposal and we can see its virtues. The central question is whether it can be agreed, legislated, financed and implemented in the foreseeable future. In view of the current problems in provincial and municipal government, can this be a process free from the influence of those with local power and wealth? Will it deliver security of tenure similar to title? Do an increasing number of landholders prefer ownership?

There are a number of alternatives, which build on existing legislation, administrative systems and expertise. The Interim Protection of Informal Land Rights Act (IPILRA) and the Prevention of Illegal Eviction Act (PIE) have been valuable pieces of legislation in protecting those with customary and informal rights against appropriation of their land. They may not have been extensively enforced but, to a limited degree, they act as deterrents. These are largely defensive Acts that are not backed up adequately by the Department of Rural Development and Land Reform. IPILRA and related Acts could be strengthened. IPILRA should be made permanent and should prioritise family or individual rights to land.

The provision allowing for dispossession by a majority 'community' decision should be deleted from legislation. If the notion of community has to be included in the Act, this should be defined as narrowly as possible: a community of landholders. Officials in the department should be trained to receive enquiries and implement the Act proactively.

At present, the majority of rural and peri-urban off-register landholders are dependent on weakly defined rights based on customary and PTO systems. Some suggest that the modified customary system is sufficiently flexible to strengthen positive rights and is developing in this direction. They argue that court judgments that take into account constitutional rights and recognise a 'living customary law' can underpin the necessary advances.

Both the Constitutional and the Land Claims Court have developed the idea of customary or indigenous ownership. This line of argument goes further to suggest that although there are examples of dispossession, most of those in the former homelands are relatively secure in the occupation of land. Customary systems are gradually enabling women to hold land independently of men. The Constitutional Court judgment in the *Bhe* case affirmed that women could inherit in customary law, and in *Jaftha* they established that land cannot be appropriated for minor debts. Although there is no longer a formal certification system, informal local records are sometimes kept that may have some value in recording land rights.

This approach, developed by lawyers associated with the Legal Resources Centre, hinges on the development of a living customary law, as recognised by the Constitutional Court, rather than attempts to fix rights in legislation.[132] Thus far, as we noted, Constitutional Court decisions have been sympathetic to socio-economic and democratic political rights of ordinary citizens. They have generally favoured the rights of individuals as against chiefs and treated men and women equally.

There are, however, potential problems with this approach. No court judgment to our knowledge specifies that family landholdings in the former homelands or in CPAs have the strength of ownership. The concept has thus far been developed at a collective level. The Constitutional Court would have to make a clear ruling in order for such protections to be secure. Until then, these rights remain uncertain and unpredictable at the same time that threats to them are becoming more widespread.

The financial benefits of controlling specific types of land provide major new incentives to drive through dispossession of customary holdings. It is dangerous for poor communities or individuals to rely on court proceedings because of the costs of going to court – they can only succeed when they get the full support of *pro bono* lawyers. Such lawyers are very stretched at a national level. Though they have been successful in some key cases, court decisions are not always followed by the executive and bureaucracy.

In addition to an urgent ruling from the Constitutional Court, it may be valuable to have a definitive essay on the customary law of immovable property by a leading lawyer to bring A.J. Kerr up to date. These two strategies seem attainable and it is possible that a partial ruling may emerge from another legal source, such as the judicial review of the Xolobeni submissions.

The emphasis on living customary law, and reliance on broad statements about the content of customary law, are also potentially problematic. Each court case on the issue requires detailed research, expert witnesses and expensive contestation. A clear ruling about the positive land rights of all off-register landholders, as families and individuals, both by Parliament and by the courts, would save a great deal of court time.

It is not certain that the courts and experts will always be sympathetic to the rights of ordinary people. Living customary law can change in the future to favour other interests. Chiefs and mining companies can find their own historians and experts. They already have an alternative narrative that has some support from government and the department. In the words of the consolidated resolutions from the Commission on the Communal Land Tenure Bill of 2016 (Eastern Cape): 'The land belongs to the various nations which are headed by a king. This system provides secure tenure for African people.' In this view, title deeds are seen as an external, white or Western way of thinking about land. Customary rights make this land inalienable, thus precluding accumulation of land by unwanted outsiders and by wealthy individuals.

Such approaches do not preclude registration or documentation of land, but protagonists argue that this should be done through traditional councils and chiefs. They should retain overall control of land allocation, repossession and administration. This system would be based on old traditional authority boundaries established during the homeland era and facilitate the extension of traditional authorities and their governance over land that is restituted. They argue that CPAs should not be created within the old Bantustan boundaries and new CPAs would be incorporated into this system. Surveys could be made of the outer boundaries of these traditional authority areas, but should not apply to the internal boundaries. Land held in this system would continue to be outside the rates and levies imposed on private property.

In our view, this system of landholding would entrench the pattern developed in the Bantustans, perpetuate the authoritarian chieftaincy of the apartheid era, and constrain the development of rural democracy. It provides little hope of unlocking agricultural production in the former homeland areas. Traditional authorities are more interested in levying income from settlements, taking rent from new settlers and using their position to become beneficiaries of investments. As in the case of the Ingonyama Trust, the temptations to increase rent are great, and this has led them to expand a form of lease that increases the income of the trust and weakens the rights of landholders.

This is the critical issue: we argue that rural policy should seek to entrench and upgrade the rights of existing landholders. Many of the cases of dispossession that we have come across involved agreement between chiefs and external agencies, whether the state or private enterprise. The necessity to include BEE partners in mining development increases the possibility that local chiefs and other powerful interests will support such development even when it requires diminishing local land rights or marginalising landholders from the benefit of development.

As in Ghana, chiefs are claiming that they are owners of the land. There may be a privatisation of customary land from above, if there is not a clear recognition of land rights from below.

A clear court judgment and legal text would underline social reality and solidify the constitutional rights to tenure security and to housing.

We are also concerned about the links between a restitution policy which is increasingly focused around the chiefs and this form of customary landholding. This is dangerous for democracy in the country and will almost certainly run counter to the constitutional principles of extending equality of rights, including gender rights. Such processes would perpetuate dualism. They seem to be the direction being offered by the now invalidated 2004 Communal Land Rights Act and, though less definitively, of the new Communal Land

Tenure Bill released in July 2017 (see below).

Our policy suggestions rest on evidence about routes that are already evident, and that seem to promise most for the economic future of South Africa and the livelihoods of rural people. We are acutely aware that many rural people wish to move to areas where employment and opportunity are greater. We believe that the opportunities to do so should be maximised in rural and urban policy, at the same time as facilitating more effective and certain forms of tenure and decentralised rural development.

We are arguing for as broad as possible recognition of existing rights and for a government policy that prioritises peri-urban private property to cater for urban migration and broaden the number of property-holders. The government should get ahead of the demographic curve to develop site-and-service titled plots of land, as well as housing, near key urban areas.

We are not arguing that everyone has the right to agricultural land. But there should be access to residential plots with gardens in the rural areas. At one stage the department was exploring the idea of one hectare per family. This seems too large and would be difficult to achieve within existing villages in many areas. Innovative approaches to water supply are particularly valuable both for household use and small-scale cultivation.

At the heart of our proposal is a recognition of very strong individual and family rights to rural residential and arable plots. Such rights grow from customary practices. There is a great deal of evidence that individual families held their land securely and that their descendants inherited their land. However, our argument – unlike that proposed in the communalist agenda – is that these rights should be recognised and formalised in court decisions and in land legislation. Full ownership and titles for this land would be an ideal solution if the issues of cost and alienability can be addressed.

Surely everyone in South Africa can support the unquestioned right of rural people – among the poorest and most vulnerable – to the specific pieces of land which they have long occupied. Their rights should be akin to ownership – whether based in customary or common law – so that they can be defended against arbitrary dispossession by chiefs and external agencies. They should be certain. By this we mean that they should not simply be cast in negative terms, as in IPILRA, but in clear positive terms.

These rights should not be secured through chiefs or other intermediaries who can use their control over allocation to build local political authority or extract rent from landholders. This applies equally to urban and peri-urban land, where informal settlements facilitate the emergence of such land and housing brokers, who are also sometimes involved in criminal enforcement practices.

The implications of this argument are gradually to build a system in which such rights can be registered. We have discussed an innovative system of registration that will not involve private title but also pointed to difficulties in its implementation.

Full titling in a single major national campaign is also unlikely to be feasible at present. However, if the existing customary rights over family land can be strongly protected in the ways that we suggest, registration at the Deeds Office can be expanded systematically. Legislation on the statute book, such as ULTRA and SPLUMA, can be amended and developed to facilitate this process, along with planning, especially in peri-urban areas and dense rural settlements.

We urgently need pilot schemes that would allow an exercise in registration and planning in the rural areas. Areas of quitrent in the Eastern Cape would be ideal sites. Deeds Office and municipal capacity also needs urgently to be enlarged to catch up with existing backlogs in titling and to expand effective registration. Expansion of ownership would require major government investment in these existing government institutions as well as support from the private sector.

We have also suggested that title deeds could include conditions and forms of ownership that would protect the interests of family members where this is required. Most families are now reduced in size and women have greater independent access to land. They are also better protected in law although the courts are not easily accessible. Women can be recorded as co-owners and, in cases where this is more difficult to specify, ownership by a single person or spouses in community of property does not preclude others sharing in some of the benefits of the property. This can be arranged by social rather than legal practices.

Conclusions and summary of recommendations

IN SUMMARY, WE ARGUE THAT tenure security and an effective restitution programme with a clear end are priorities for South Africa. The threats to customary/PTO land have increased in recent years and the protections are insufficient.

Landholdings are a major asset for many of South Africa's poorest families and they should not be elbowed aside in the development of rural areas. Equally they need strong rights in cities and peri-urban areas. If there is not a cementing of rights from below, then there may be a privatisation from above. It has already begun in some mining zones.

We have suggested a series of practical, attainable policies that will accomplish the following:
- Continue to provide poor families with access to residential land in the urban and rural areas.
- Strengthen rights of existing landholders in customary/PTO tenure areas. Family or individual landholdings should be 'akin to ownership'.
- Amend IPILRA in order to strengthen the protections for family and individual landholdings. Provide effective implementation.

CONCLUSIONS AND SUMMARY

- Facilitate upgrading of land rights to title, starting in the urban and densely settled peri-urban areas.
- Urgently develop pilot tenure projects that test the feasibility and cost of the Land Records idea, the community choice options offered in the Communal Land Tenure Bill and the expansion of rural ownership. Our argument and evidence suggest the value of developing one flexible system of ownership throughout the country. Connect these developments with planning for services.
- Experiment with pilot projects for the reconfiguration of rural settlements in order to facilitate the creation of consolidated landholdings for farming.
- Resolve the backlog of over one million in registration of titles for RDP houses and update the existing titles.
- Invest in government capacity to register and administer land.
- Restore the original aims of restitution and ensure that claims are fully researched and fairly settled. Where possible, unbundle large chiefly-led claims.
- Appoint an effective research panel for restitution claims and appoint permanent judges to the Land Claims Court until restitution is complete.
- Prioritise cash payments for restitution.
- Ideally the Restitution Amendment Act of 2014 should not go forward. It is an ill-considered act, motivated by short-term political considerations, that will cause uncertainty in the countryside, undermine agricultural production and provide little effective base for rural development for the recipients of land.
- Pursue instead a gradual programme of redistribution that prioritises production and rural development both for existing and new landholders.

- Land tenure and redistribution policy must take central account of the need for mobility and the realities of rapid urbanisation.

Appendix

Comments on the Communal Land Tenure Bill, 2017[133]

AFTER WE HAD COMPLETED this text, the government published a new Bill on communal tenure in July 2017. This proposed legislation is very wide-ranging and aims to cater for all off-register land, including the former homelands and land transferred to African communities since 1994. It is a potentially flexible measure that attempts to open up a number of different scenarios for tenure on communal land. In addition, it offers different outcomes in regard to the administration of that land.

The Bill directly addresses the key clause, section 25(6) in the Constitution of 1996, which required the government to provide 'legally secure tenure' as well as section 25(5) specifying that the state must take reasonable measures 'to foster conditions which enable citizens to gain access to land on an equitable basis'.

At the heart of this Bill is the fundamental dilemma that we have addressed about the future of land tenure in South Africa. Should communal or customary forms of landholding be protected and expanded? Or should private property gradually be expanded to cover the country as a whole. The Bill seems to allow for both directions through choice by local communities. However, this decision has to be made by a 60 per cent majority of an unspecified local community, rather than by individual landholders, and thus the legislation may favour communalist or traditionalist approaches.

Land rights inquiry, determination and community
The Bill attempts to deal with two levels of landholding simultaneously: community-held and individually held land. It recognises the social realities of many communal/customary areas in which individual holdings and rights intersect with those of wider groupings. For example, individuals hold residential and arable plots, while a broader grouping, called a community in the Bill, may regulate grazing and other common land to which individuals have access. Individuals may not be able to protect their arable lands from livestock throughout the year.

A major problem with the Bill is that the first step in enhancing tenure is to extend community or collective ownership, registered at the Deeds Office, rather than to start with individuals or families.

Before any changes are made in landholding, certain procedures are necessary. It is unclear whether these have to be initiated by the Department of Rural Development and Land Reform or communities themselves, and whether these are compulsory for every off-register community.

Following the decision to begin the process, the department appoints a 'land rights inquirer'. This can either be a departmental official or another person; assistants can also be appointed. If they are not members of the department, they will be paid. The inquirer liaises between the community and the department, and assesses 'the nature and extent of land rights' as well as the options for ensuring secure tenure. The enquiry must be publicised in the media, 'inviting interested parties' with a time deadline. The inquirer must take written or verbal evidence and convene meetings. At the end of the process, the findings must be made public.

At this point, the minister, after consulting the community, and resolving any disputes, makes a *determination* of the land to be transferred to the community and individuals in that community. Some of the land can be reserved for the state in consultation with the local municipality.

A critical issue concerns the geographic extent and nature of a community, which we have addressed in another context in chapter 10. In section 1 of the Bill, on definitions, 'community means a group of persons whose rights to land are derived from shared rules determining access to land held in common by such a group regardless of its ethnic, tribal, religious or racial identity and includes a traditional community'. This is helpful in the sense that it excludes communities defined by identity and seems to lay emphasis on geographical communities – that is, people who live in the same area. The wording also follows the guidelines developed in the judgments by Moseneke and others, discussed in chapter 12. However, the inclusion of traditional community may be contradictory or at least paradoxical here. Is someone who regards themselves as a member of a traditional community, but lives outside the area in which 'shared rules' are accepted, a member of the community for the purposes of the Bill? Are they and their descendants entitled to land there by virtue of that identity?

The Bill does not specify the geographical extent of a community for the purposes of landownership. Is the community with shared rules intended to mean a group settled within an existing political boundary, such as a municipality, district, ward or a village? Sections of the Bill seem to suggest that, despite the definition above, a community can be a traditional council recognised under the Traditional Leadership and Governance Framework Act (2003). These units may not coincide with other geographic units, and if they are recognised as communities, then the forms of tenure and administration are more likely to come under the influence or control of traditional authorities. For example, the Zulu Ingonyama Trust may try to keep control over the whole area currently under its authority – that is, all of the former KwaZulu homeland plus some transferred farms.

How small a group can act as a community for the purposes of the Bill? For example, in Transkeian administrative areas, formerly under the administrative authority of a headman, there can be ten or more villages. The basic 'shared rules' about management of land are partly developed at this village level of perhaps a couple of hundred families. Can a village act as a community? Can a cluster of ten families living in the same area who wish to have 'shared rules', expressed as private rights to their land, apply to the department separately from a larger group around them that might wish to follow customary or communal practices?

Quitrent or individual Glen Grey holdings in the Eastern Cape have in theory been upgraded to private title. But some of these exist within areas where there are also former PTO sites. Which 'shared rules' will shape the community in this area?

Starting with such an imprecise notion of community will result in a great deal of confusion and conflict in the implementation of such policies and make them vulnerable to capture by local elites. Our view is that it is better to start with existing individual/family landholders and restrict ownership to that level. Communities or wider groupings should be restricted to administrative responsibilities. As we noted in chapter 3, the ULTRA legislation already provides for such upgrading.

Ownership and individuals
Section 11 specifies that following the determination – that is, the detailed assessment of land rights – and resolution of any disputes, the community receives a title deed of communally owned land. It then has to meet in order to decide what kind of tenure it prefers for the individual landholders in respect of residential, agricultural, industrial or commercial plots. Communities can choose individual ownership, or a form of lease, or a more communal arrangement in which ownership will rest with the community alone, and individuals will only have rights to use land. Women will have equal rights to occupy and own land in community-owned areas; it is very important to have legal clarity on this point, confirming both the Constitution and a gradually expanding practice. The Bill does not seem to make provision for family ownership or co-ownership. An indirect exception in section 13 gives families some rights of consultation before sale.

The Bill seems to guarantee that individual landholders will have secure use rights, even where a community does not allow for individual ownership. Similar provisions apply to state-owned land on which individuals are settled. This is an important provision because the government appears to be holding onto some land that has been bought for the purposes of land reform and then leasing it out or allowing use rather than ownership; some security is extended to those on government-owned land.

If secure legal rights cannot be provided, then landholders are entitled to 'comparable redress' or compensation.

Sections 26 and 27 describe the procedures by which these key decisions are made. Community rules must be adopted by a 60 per cent majority of households, not 60 per cent of holders of agricultural land. The great majority of households will have residential plots, but they will not all have arable plots, and this is a provision that might also tend to favour communal rather than private tenure of agricultural land. Rules may allow for ownership of some kinds of land at the same time as asserting community ownership and control over common areas. The agreed rules must be set down and submitted to the department and are 'binding on the entire community'. Decisions need to be made by inclusive and democratic processes.

If a community chooses to give ownership of subdivided portions of land to the landholders, then that individual becomes owner and receives a separate title deed. Ownership can, however, be constrained by conditions and community rules. This includes constraints on the sale of land, which, as we signalled above, in chapter 4, can be a contentious question. Under section 13(a) communal land cannot be 'sold, donated, leased, encumbered or in any manner disposed of without a written resolution to that effect supported by 60 per cent of households of the relevant community'. In section 13(b) a subdivided portion of the communal land cannot be sold or donated to a person 'who is not a member of that community' without the consent of the owner's family as well as members of the community and the state. Thus the Bill entrenches significant legal restrictions on ownership and alienation by the owner's family. It also restricts sale outside 'members of the relevant community' and hence – as noted

APPENDIX

above – lays particular significance on precision in legally defining a member of the community. Would it not be better to word this in a different way and simply talk of an individual landholder and not a community member – a concept that is very difficult to specify?

This clause is clearly designed to restrict any purchase by corporate entities or outsiders unless there is widespread local agreement. The result is a restricted version of ownership and of a land market, yet in many communal areas there are already transactions in land. While we see the value in such an approach, it will be difficult to enforce. A form of family or co-ownership may be more effective.

Sections 9 and 17 provide that a 'general plan' or a land use plan must be developed that outlines the areas to be designated for subdivision and for other uses including services and conservation. A survey is also needed.

Following these processes, further land registration at the Deeds Office is required for all the individually held subdivisions of land. If we have understood the text, each of these must be registered in the name of the owner where private tenure has been chosen. If the community decides that it will only give rights to individuals to use or lease land, then the subdivided pieces of land must be registered in the name of both the community and the community member. The costs of this initial registration must be paid by the department – this provision follows the precedent set in the Upgrading of Land Tenure Acts of 1991 and 1998.

In a confusing provision, however, section 29,1(c) appears to require additionally a local register of land rights and of transactions affecting such rights. This certainly needs to be clarified, and it is unclear whether and why two registers are needed and how records will be kept. Will there be national rules with electronic records that can be made available locally? A separate local register is surely a problem because many local communities may not have the means and skills to keep a land register, and there are likely to be discrepancies between the local and national registers unless there is one electronic record.

The Bill aims to 'enable access to land on an equitable basis' and section 5,7(c) provides that before a determination is made, consideration should be given to 'the need to provide access to land on an equitable basis'. This formulation derives directly from clause 25(5) in the Bill of Rights in the Constitution. However, it is unclear which kind of land is referred to. Although there is a great deal of variation, at present many settlements in the former homelands are divided into residential areas with gardens, arable plots (generally held only by a minority) and grazing commonage to which most households have access. The last is usually the biggest area except in larger dense settlements.

Does this provision refer to residential land only or to all three categories of land? Is the implication that all members of a community should have equal access to arable plots? The arable plot sizes are already too small for successful mechanised farming and they are largely unused in most villages at present. Our view is that every family should have a right to a residential plot (including a garden) but not to agricultural land.

Administration, costs and competencies
In addition to the far-reaching involvement of the department in every land determination, in every land use plan and land-owning community, the Bill proposes three layers of land administration.

APPENDIX

Firstly, sections 28 and 29 provide that once registered as landowners, communities must decide within 24 months by a 60 per cent majority to hold their land through a CPA or a traditional council or any other approved entity. These bodies must provide general management and administration, maintain registers, resolve disputes, facilitate the extension of municipal functions and services, and oversee development. They must meet at least four times a year and submit an annual report to the department.

Secondly, section 32 provides that the community must establish a 'Households Forum' of between 20 and 30 members including an elected chair and at least 50 per cent women. They will be the vehicle for day-to-day management of land, receiving and making reports, administering the rules, and updating the registers. However, they seem to be separate from the CPA or traditional council and not to be a subcommittee of these bodies that will own the community land.

Thirdly, sections 36–39 provide for Communal Land Boards of 9–15 members, including one from the provincial House of Traditional Leaders, one from the department, one from the municipality and at least five representing communities. These are advisory boards monitoring and assisting implementation and the resolution of disputes. They also report to the minister, and members will receive payment if not employed by the state.

In addition to these three layers of administration, municipalities also have significant functions in relation to planning and services that impinge on the administration of land.

The department will finance all of these layers of administration.

This administrative structure seems too complex with too many layers and it is unlikely to work effectively. Perhaps the aim of the Households Forum is to ensure a democratic and popular counterweight to the communal owners – the traditional council or CPA. But this is likely to create conflicts of authority. The CPAs and traditional council should themselves be representative and democratic. Creating new collective bodies for ownership will in itself produce significant problems for decision-making – as is evident in the existing CPAs. It is difficult for them to make decisions or to initiate innovations and investment. Creating an additional collective body for administration will compound the problem.

The Communal Land Boards create another layer of authority and interest that is likely to confuse the position further. The fact that their members are paid may well be resented by communities. Conflict resolution is surely better done through those who have become immersed in the details of the original determination and land use plans – the land inquirers and departmental officials. In the last resort, the courts rather than a land board would surely be the best venue to resolve intractable conflict because they alone have the authority to make such judgments.

One overarching local administrative body should administer (but not own) collective interests and any shared resources. They should be set up within defined political boundaries and not as communities.

General comments
This legislation seems to create major new demands on the department, to lead to over-localisation of decision-making, to prioritise community ownership over secure individual

ownership, and to introduce too many layers of local administration over land.

Surely pilot schemes in each province should be attempted before the Bill is enacted. It has taken over twenty years to develop this legislation and yet it has not been tried out. Implementation is likely to take many years. In the interim, the main aim of the Bill, legally secure landholding, has to be effectively realised through other routes, including the enforcement of existing legislation such as IPILRA, the clarification of customary law, and the extension and amendment of ULTRA.

The Bill may not even be effective in providing legal security for existing individual/family landholdings because its primary focus seems to be on creating community ownership. This may provide protection from external threats to land. But, as we have noted, many of the threats to family landholdings come from elements in communities working with outside agents. Is it necessary to make communities the owners of land? We have indicated that we do not think that traditional councils should own land. Surely this should be reserved for the landholders and the Bill should concentrate on protecting the land rights of individuals/families.

Land rights inquiries of the type envisaged at community and individual level are very time-consuming and require considerable skills and resources that are unlikely to be available in the department. Opening up the issue of community boundaries for the purpose of ownership could be conflictual and slow the process.

The department will need to deal with thousands, maybe tens of thousands, of complex land inquiries, on a scale similar to the restitution process. Is the state ready for this? A new sub-department with well-trained staff will be needed. Detailed on-the-ground research in far-flung rural areas will be needed; this together with dispute resolution may be demanding, labour-intensive and time-consuming. It may be costly if land inquirers are paid. The Bill could not be implemented without a major departmental expansion that will require funding and careful preparation.

The Deeds Office, which falls under the Department of Rural Development and Land Reform, will also require expansion and additional training of officials to deal with millions of new registrations – effectively a doubling in size. It is reported that there is already a backlog of over a million titles resulting from RDP housing grants, and this needs to be cleared first.

The department is apparently going to contribute to the conveyancing required for registrations, as well as surveying tasks and land use plans. Once land is registered, state assistance will be required to keep the records up to date. Servicing the complicated local land administration system will also take departmental time and energy. Successful implementation of a Bill of this kind will require huge expansion of skilled bureaucrats.

It is true that we have advocated expansion of the Deeds Office and surveying capacity to deal with additional registrations, but our recommendations focus more on individual/family landholdings rather than this dual system of community and individual ownership together with multi-layered administration.

The Bill lacks clarity as to the sequence of implementation and the timing of various stages. The sequence can only really be tested through practice, and this uncertainty underlines the need for pilot implementation before the Bill is passed.

Section 46 notes that the minister may 'acquire more land

or a right in land for use as communal land to ensure access to land on an equitable basis'. This is already provided for in the redistribution programme.

If it is to be land for farming, then there is strong argument that the state needs first to resolve the collapse of agricultural production in the existing communal lands before extending this form of ownership. Land held in private ownership by individuals or corporations has, despite the removal of most subsidies, continued to be the base for most productive agriculture in the country. Residential sites should be provided in the rural areas where needed, and prioritised in urban zones.

Endnotes

1. Department of Rural Development and Land Reform, notice 510 of 2017, *Government Gazette*, 7 July 2017.
2. Department of Rural Development and Land Reform, Annual Report of the Commission on Restitution of Land Rights, 2015–16 reported 143,000 new claims but media reports noted 160,000 by July 2016 when the Constitutional Court ruling was made.
3. Gugile Nkwinti, Department of Rural Development and Land Reform Budget proposal, 2017; Wandile Sihlobo and Tinashe Kapuya, 'Land policies try to solve imaginary issues at expense of real problems', *Business Day*, 6 June 2017. They probably exaggerate land transfers but others such as John Kane-Berman also suggest that black landholdings are now over 30 per cent.
4. STATSSA, Mid-Year Population Estimates 2016.
5. Gavin Capps and Sonwabile Mnwana, 'Claims from below: Platinum and the politics of land in the Bakgatla-ba-Kgafela traditional authority area', *Review of African Political Economy*, 42 (2015), 606–624.
6. Gavin Capps and Stanley Malindi, 'Dealing with the tribe: The politics of the Bapo/Lonmin royalty-to-equity conversion', Working Paper 8, Society, Work and Development Institute (SWOP), University of the Witwatersrand.
7. Peter Delius, with Rosalie Kingwill and Matthew Chaskalson, 'A historical investigation of underlying rights to land registered as state owned', Unpublished paper for the Tenure Reform Core Group, Department of Land Affairs, 1997.

ENDNOTES

8 Donna Hornby, Rosalie Kingwill, Lauren Royston and Ben Cousins (eds), *Untitled: Securing Land Tenure in Urban and Rural South Africa*, Pietermaritzburg: University of KwaZulu-Natal Press, 2017.
9 Aninka Claassens and Ben Cousins (eds), *Land, Power and Custom*, Cape Town: Juta, 2008.
10 William Beinart, Peter Delius and Stanley Trapido (eds.), *Putting a Plough to the Ground*, Johannesburg: Ravan Press, 1986.
11 Alastair J. Kerr, *The Customary Law of Immovable Property and of Succession*, Grahamstown: Grocott and Sherry, 1990; Peter Delius, 'Contested terrain: Land rights and chiefly power in historical perspective' in Claassens and Cousins (eds), *Land, Power and Custom*, pp. 218–221.
12 Eileen Krige, 'Note on the Phalaborwa and their Morula complex', *Bantu Studies*, 11, 1 (1937), 362.
13 Monica Hunter, *Reaction to Conquest: Effects of Contact with Europeans on the Pondo of South Africa*, London: Oxford University Press, 1964, p. 113.
14 Delius, 'Contested terrain'.
15 T.W. Bennett, *Customary Law in South Africa*, Cape Town: Juta, 2004.
16 Geoff Budlender and Johan Latsky, 'Unravelling rights to land in rural race zones', in M. de Klerk (ed.), *A Harvest of Discontent: The Land Question in South Africa*, Cape Town: IDASA, 1991, pp. 115–138.
17 William Beinart, *Twentieth-Century South Africa*, Oxford: Oxford University Press, 2001, p. 211.
18 Union of South Africa, Betterment Areas Proclamation, 116 of 1949.
19 Mcintosh, Xaba and Associates, *Land Issues Scoping Study: Communal Land Tenure Areas* (2003), available at: www.sarpn.org/documents/d0000646/P657-DFID.pdf, accessed in June 2017 p. 12.
20 Debbie Budlender, 'Women, marriage and land: Findings from a three-site survey', *Acta Juridica*, (2013), 28–48.
21 Interviews by William Beinart and Luvuyo Wotshela in preparation for the Mgungundhlovu restitution case, Bizana, Eastern Cape.

22 Summary obtained from Mike Coleman, former departmental officer, Eastern Cape Department of Land Affairs, 2017.
23 Rosalie Kingwill, 'An ethnography of land title in the Eastern Cape', *Kronos*, 40 (2014), 241–268.
24 Ingonyama Trust Board, Annual Report, 2013–14, Briefing to the Portfolio Committee on Rural Development and Land Reform, 15 October 2014; Mbongiseni Buthelezi and Stha Yeni, 'Traditional leadership in democratic South Africa: Pitfalls and prospects', Unpublished paper.
25 Philile Ntuli, 'Whose land is it anyway?', Presentation to the conference on Land and Contested Histories, LARC, University of Cape Town, 2016.
26 Siyabulela Manona, '"Informal" land rights under siege 18 years into democracy', Draft paper presented to Rural Women Action Research Project (RWAR), University of Cape Town, March 2012, www.cls.uct.ac.za/usr/lrg/downloads/Manona_DraftSeminarPaper_March2012.pdf, accessed in June 2017; Bronwen Viedge, 'A history of land tenure in the Herschel district, Transkei', MA, Rhodes University, 2001.
27 Thanks to Aninka Claassens for providing this judgment.
28 Churchill Guduza, 'Housing markets in Greater Soweto', PhD, London School of Economics, 1997.
29 Umhlaba Rural Services, 'Situational analysis of the upgrading of Land Tenure Rights Act (ULTRA)', 2009. Jean du Plessis, team leader and primary author.
30 Interviews by Beinart and Wotshela of Mrs Joe, Deeds Office, KWT, and Johann Badenhorst, retired Registrar of Deeds, 28 February 2017.
31 Tara Weinberg, 'Contesting customary law in the Eastern Cape: gender, place and land tenure', *Acta Juridica*, (2013) 100–117.
32 Deborah James, *Money from Nothing: Indebtedness and Aspiration in South Africa*, Stanford: Stanford University Press, 2015, pp. 178–180.
33 Luvuyo Wotshela, 'Quitrent tenure and the village system in the former Ciskei region of the Eastern Cape: Implications for contemporary land reform of a century of social change', *Journal of Southern African Studies*, 40, 4 (2014), 727–744.

34 Umhlaba Rural Services, 'Situational analysis', has a detailed analysis of Mgwali.
35 On CPAs, see Deborah James, *Gaining Ground: 'Rights' and 'Property' in South African Land Reform*, Abingdon: Routledge-Cavendish, 2007; Donna Hornby, 'Analysis of the Communal Properties Amendment Bill', Association for Rural Advancement, Pietermaritzburg, 2016.
36 Hornby, Kingwill, Royston and Cousins, *Untitled*, p. 6.
37 James, *Money from Nothing*.
38 Khumisho Moguerane, 'A home of their own', Paper written for this project.
39 Budlender, 'Women, marriage and land'.
40 Personal communication, Hannah Dawson, DPhil student, University of Oxford.
41 Matthew de la Hey and William Beinart, 'Why have South African smallholders largely abandoned arable production in fields? A case study', *Journal of Southern African Studies*, 43, 4 (2017), 753–770.
42 James Fenske, 'Land tenure and investment incentives: Evidence from West Africa', *Journal of Development Economics*, 95, 2 (2011), 137–156.
43 Haydn J. Brooks, 'The role of field and garden cultivation for food security under a changing climate: The case of Fairbairn and Ntloko villages, Eastern Cape', MSc, Rhodes University, 2017.
44 Jeff Peires, 'The legend of Fenner Solomon' in B. Bozzoli (ed.), *Class, Community and Conflict: South African Perspectives*, Johannesburg: Ravan Press, 1987, pp. 65–92.
45 Janine M. Ubink and Kojo S. Amanor (eds), *Contesting Land and Custom in Ghana: State, Chief and the Citizen*, Amsterdam: Amsterdam University Press, 2009.
46 Michael Barry and Jennifer Whittal, 'Land registration effectiveness in a state-subsidised housing project in Mbekweni, South Africa', *Land Use Policy*, 56 (2016), 197–208.
47 Kingwill, 'An ethnography of land title'.
48 Mary Tiffen, Michael Mortimore and Francis Gichuki, *More People, Less Erosion: Environmental Recovery in Kenya*, Chichester: Wiley, 1994.
49 Aninka Claassens and Dee Smythe (eds), *Acta Juridica*, (2013),

special issue on 'Marriage Law and Custom'.
50   Interviews by Beinart and Wotshela, and case materials.
51   Martin Adams, Ben Cousins and Siyabulela Manona, 'Land tenure and economic development in rural South Africa: Constraints and opportunities', Working paper 125, Overseas Development Institute, 1999, p. 15.
52   These paragraphs on the idea of a Land Records Act are taken from a memorandum submitted by Siyabu Manona and Rosalie Kingwill to the parliamentary High Level Panel on Land and from Rosalie Kingwill's paper for the project on 'Land tenure in South Africa: Current protection for off-register rights and a proposal to enhance security of tenure'. Background arguments are in Hornby, Kingwill, Royston and Cousins, *Untitled*.
53   Hornby, Kingwill, Royston and Cousins, *Untitled*, pp. 80–81.
54   Department of Rural Development and Land Reform, 'The Communal Land Tenure Policy Framework', 2014, www.ruraldevelopment.gov.za/publications/communal-land-indaba-2015/file/3530-commission-01-communal-land-tenure-policy-framework, accessed in June 2017.
55   Derick Fay, '"The trust is over! We want to plough!": Social differentiation and the reversal of resettlement in South Africa', *Human Ecology*, 40, 1 (2012), 59–68.
56   De la Hey and Beinart, 'South African smallholders'.
57   Tiffen, Mortimore and Gichuki, *More People, Less Erosion*.
58   Visit by Beinart and Wotshela, 2017.
59   Yves van Leynseele, 'Landscapes of deracialisation: Power, brokerage and place-making on a South African frontier', PhD, Wageningen University, 2013; Tshililo Manenzhe, 'Agrarian change and the fate of farmworkers: Trajectories of strategic partnership and farm labour in Levubu Valley, South Africa', PhD, University of the Western Cape, 2015.
60   This section is based largely on Beinart's work as an expert witness in three cases which we will call *Hlolweni*, *Mgungundhlovu* and *Xolobeni*. His understanding of the issues has benefitted greatly from discussion with the lawyers leading the cases, particularly Alan Dodson, Susannah Cowen and Henk Smith.
61   *Bakgatla-ba-Kgafela Communal Property Association* vs *Bakgatla-*

ENDNOTES

ba-Kgafela Tribal Authority and Others [2015] ZACC 25.
62 Aninka Claassens, 'Denying ownership and equal citizenship: Continuities in the state's use of law and "custom", 1913–2013', *Journal of Southern African Studies*, 40, 4 (2014), 761–779.
63 Edward Lahiff, 'Land tenure in South Africa's communal areas: A case study of the Arabie-Olifants scheme', *African Studies*, 59, 1 (2000), 50.
64 Barbara Oomen, *Chiefs in South Africa: Land, Power and Culture in the Post-Apartheid Era*, Oxford: James Currey, 2005.
65 Michelle Hay and Ripfumelo Mushwana, 'Customary land tenure in Mopani district today and what it suggests about land titling', Unpublished paper for this project. Both have researched on land issues in the district before.
66 Documents in possession of Michelle Hay.
67 Michelle Hay (MH) and Ripfumelo Mushwana (RM), interview with Respondent T, 26 July 2016.
68 MH and RM interview with Respondent A, 7 July 2016.
69 RM interview with Respondent G, 13 July 2016.
70 MH and RM interview with Respondent T, 26 July 2016.
71 Moguerane, 'A home of their own'.
72 MH interview with Respondent H, 15 July 2016.
73 RM interview with Respondent M, 20 July 2016.
74 MH and RM interview with Respondent W, 26 July 2016.
75 Lahiff, 'Land tenure', p. 59.
76 Interview with Norah Mlondobozi, 5 August 2016.
77 Scott Drimie and Laura Pereira, 'Advances in food security and sustainability in South Africa', in David Barling (ed.), *Advances in Food Security and Sustainability*, vol. 1, Amsterdam: Academic Press, 2016, pp. 1–31.
78 The section is based on in-depth research by Delius and Hay on restitution over the last decade. Michelle Hay's doctoral thesis, 'South Africa's land reform in historical perspective', University of the Witwatersrand, 2015, provided key insights as did the series of research reports mentioned in notes below. Over the last year, Delius and Hay have also produced a report and recommendations on restitution for the parliamentary High Level Panel. This has benefitted from extended discussion with Alan Dodson and

Shirhami Shirinda and incorporates their perspectives.
79 John Wright, 'Turbulent times: Political transformations in the north and east, 1760s–1830s' in Caroline Hamilton, Bernard K. Mbenga and Robert Ross, *The Cambridge History of South Africa, vol. 1, From Early Times to 1885*, Cambridge: Cambridge University Press, 2012.
80 Martin Chanock, *The Making of South African Legal Culture 1902–1936: Fear, Favour and Prejudice*, Cambridge: Cambridge University Press, 2001.
81 Peter Delius, *The Land Belongs to Us*, Berkeley: University of California Press, 1984, pp. 14–17.
82 Hunter, *Reaction to Conquest*, p. 113.
83 See the White Paper on Land Reform, 1997.
84 Cherryl Walker, *Landmarked: Land Claims and Land Restitution in South Africa*, Johannesburg: Jacana Media, 2008, pp. 16–17.
85 Deborah James, '"After years in the wilderness": The discourse of land claims in the new South Africa', *Journal of Peasant Studies*, 27, 3 (2000), 142–161.
86 Peter Delius, *A Lion Amongst the Cattle*, Johannesburg: Ravan Press, 1996, p. 224.
87 Walker, *Landmarked*, chs. 1 and 2.
88 Walker, *Landmarked*, pp. 36–39.
89 Peter Delius, Michelle Hay, Ross Douglas and Nicholas Leontsinis, 'Report on the historical validity of land claims by the Moletele community and others concerning farms in the Maruleng region', Unpublished report, 2014.
90 Peter Delius and Michelle Hay, 'Report on claims lodged by various communities in the Sabi Sands Area', Unpublished report, 2013.
91 The Minister of Land Affairs, Mr Derek Hanekom: Press Briefing: Information on Land Reform Programme, 23 February 1995, available at www.gov.za, accessed in 2014.
92 Cherryl Walker, 'Finite land: Challenges institutionalising land restitution in South Africa, 1995–2000', *Journal of Southern African Studies*, 38, 4 (2012), 809–826.
93 Walker, 'Finite land', p. 813.
94 Walker, 'Finite land', p. 819.

95 Walker, 'Finite land', p. 823.
96 Edward Lahiff, 'The impact of land reform policy in the Northern Province' in Ben Cousins (ed.), *At the Crossroads: Land and Agrarian Reform in South Africa into the 21st Century*, Bellville: Programme for Land and Agrarian Studies (PLAAS), University of the Western Cape and National Land Committee (NLC), 2000, p. 102.
97 See Hay, 'South Africa's land reform in historical perspective', pp. 232–234.
98 Lahiff, 'The impact of land reform', p. 98; see also James, *Gaining Ground*, p. 205.
99 James, *Gaining Ground*.
100 James, *Gaining Ground*, ch. 2.
101 Walker, *Landmarked*.
102 Walker, *Landmarked*, p. 15.
103 Hay, 'South Africa's land reform in historical perspective', pp. 237–238.
104 Nkuzi Development Association, Annual Report, 2002.
105 See Hay, 'Land reform in historical perspective', pp. 263–271 for a fuller discussion.
106 To understand the context in which decisions to merge claims were taken, and examples of different cases, see D. James, 'Burial sites, informal rights, and lost kingdoms: Contesting land claims in Mpumalanga, South Africa', *Africa*, 79, 2 (2009), 228–251.
107 The following section on the implications of certain court judgments for land restitution also draws on a very informative discussion with Alan Dodson. See Judgment by Dodson, J., *Kranspoort Community Re: Farm Kranspoort* 48 LS Land Claims Court case 26/98 [1999] ZALCC 67 (10 December 1999), available at www.saflii.org/za/cases/ZALCC/1999/67.html.
108 Hansi Mostert, 'Change through jurisprudence: The role of the courts in broadening the scope of restitution' in Cherryl Walker, Anna Bohlin, Ruth Hall and Lungisile Kepe (eds.), *Land, Memory, Reconstruction, and Justice: Perspectives on Land Claims in South Africa*, Athens: Ohio University Press, 2010.
109 See judgment by Moseneke, Deputy Chief Justice, *Department of Land Affairs and Others* vs *Goedgelegen Tropical Fruits (Pty) Ltd*,

Constitutional Court of South Africa, Case 69/06 [2007] ZACC 12; 2007 (10) BCLR 1027 (CC); 2007 (6) SA 199 (CC) (6 June 2007), available at www.saflii.org/za/cases/ZACC/2007/12.html.

110 The commission also ignored two judgments of the Land Claims Court that expressly and directly say that you cannot artificially create a community by merging communities or by merging claims. There are the *Bouvest* and *Minaar* judgments. See, for text reference, judgment by Dodson, J., Kranspoort Community Re: Farm Kranspoort 48 LS, Land Claims Court case 26/98 [1999] ZALCC 67 (10 December 1999), available at www.saflii.org/za/cases/ZALCC/1999/67.html.

111 Authors' calculations based on the following sources: CRLR presentation to Parliament, 19 August 2013 (available at: www.pmg.org.za/committee-meeting/16204/); Commission for the Restitution of Land Rights Annual Reports 2013/14; 2014/15, 2015/16; News brief from Commission for the Restitution of Land Rights; www.ruraldevelopment.gov.za/news-room/news-flash/file/5169; Commission for the Restitution of Land Rights, Annual Performance Plan 2016/17, pp. 20–21.

112 CRLR Strategic Plan 2015–2020, and Annual Performance Plan 2015/2016, p. 11.

113 Alan Dodson, 'Flawed marriages, difficult divorces: Conflict in land trusts and CPAs', Unpublished paper presented at the Contested Histories Workshop, June 2016; Ben Cousins and Cherryl Walker (eds.), *Land Divided, Land Restored: Land Reform in South Africa for the 21st Century*, Johannesburg: Jacana Media, 2015; Walker et al. *Land, Memory*; Ruth Hall and Lungisile Ntsebeza (eds.), *The Land Question in South Africa: The Challenge of Transformation and Redistribution*, Cape Town: HSRC Press, 2007.

114 Pearlie Joubert and Stephan Hofstatter, 'Government to pay R1 billion for Mala Mala game reserve', *Timeslive*, 4 August 2013, available at: www.timeslive.co.za/politics/2013/08/04/government-to-pay-r1-billion-for-mala-mala-game-reserve.

115 Joubert and Hofstatter, 'Government to pay R1 billion for Mala Mala game reserve'.

116 Elise Tempelhoff, 'Oudhoof van parke se belange botsend', *Die Beeld*, 7 April 2015: 'David Mabunda glo R81 m. ryker ná grondeis'.

ENDNOTES

117 This section is based on Hay, 'Land reform in historical perspective', pp. 263–271. See also Marj Brown, Justin Erasmus, Rosalie Kingwill, Colin Murray and Monty Roodt, 'Land restitution in South Africa: An independent evaluation', Manchester: Institute for Development Policy and Management, 1997, pp. 22–24; Bill Derman, Edward Lahiff and Espen Sjaastad, 'Strategic questions about strategic partners: Challenges and pitfalls in South Africa's new model of land restitution' in Walker et al., *Land, Memory.*

118 Brown et al, 'Land restitution in South Africa'; James, '"After years in the wilderness"', pp. 142–161; James, *Gaining Ground*; Derick Fay and Deborah James, 'Giving back land or righting wrongs? Comparative issues in the study of land restitution' in Walker et al., *Land, Memory.*

119 Bernadette Atuahene, *We Want What's Ours: Learning from South Africa's Land Restitution Programme*, Oxford: Oxford University Press, 2014, ch. 4.

120 Nomalanga Mkhize, 'New land restitution process set to be messy', *Business Day Live*, 15 July 2014, available at www.bdlive.co.za/opinion/columnists/2014/07/15/new-land-restitution-process-set-to-be-messy, accessed 15 July 2014.

121 Hay, 'South Africa's land reform in historical perspective'; D. Skosana, 'Community views on the Restitution of Land Rights Amendment Bill, Report 1', Unpublished report commissioned by the Centre for Law and Society, November 2013, p. 9.

122 ANC Member of Parliament, name unknown, public hearing on the 2013 Restitution of Land Rights Amendment Bill, Moses Mabatha Civic Centre, Sekhukhune district, Limpopo, 19 November 2013.

123 ANC Member of Parliament, name unknown, public hearing on the 2013 Restitution of Land Rights Amendment Bill, p. 16.

124 'Land Restitution Amendment Bill: Minister of Rural Development & Commission for Restitution of Land Rights responses to public submissions', 3 February 2014, available at: www.pmg.org.za, accessed 19 February 2014.

125 William Beinart, 'Verwoerd, Zuma and the chiefs', www.customcontested.co.za/verwoerd-zuma-chiefs/ , accessed in June 2017.

126 'Short history', document in our possession, p. 15.
127 Adam Kuper, 'The return of the native', *Current Anthropology*, 44, 3 (2003), 390.
128 Tammy Petersen, 'South Africa: Fight for land worth dying for', 10 December 2015, available at: www.allafrica.com/stories/201512110669.html, accessed September 2016.
129 www.youtube.com/playlist?list=PLt0wwMdzvHOq_Z7hR_cKZbvv4PcM-LZVR, accessed May 2017.
130 The recommendations that are set out below have been developed by Peter Delius, Alan Dodson, Michelle Hay and Shirhami Shirinda in the course of preparing inputs for the High Level Panel chaired by Kgalema Motlanthe.
131 See Judgment by Gildenhuys, J., Kusile Land Committee, Land Claims Court, Case LCC21/07(2014).
132 Wilmien Wicomb, 'Securing women's customary rights in land: The fallacy of institutional recognition', *Acta Juridica*, (2013) 49–72; Geoff Budlender, 'Opportunities for constitutional jurisprudence and its development', Unpublished paper given at the Contested Histories workshop, LARC, University of Cape Town, 2016.
133 Department of Rural Development and Land Reform, notice 510 of 2017, *Government Gazette*, 7 July 2017.

Index

A

Adams, Martin 52
African National Congress
  (ANC) 1, 3, 12, 26–7, 34, 95,
  99, 109
agricultural land 2, 17, 28, 46–7,
  82–3, 113, 165
  black landholdings 5
  investment in 91
  livestock practices 65
  private tenure of 165
  small-scale farmers 87
*Alexkor vs Richtersveld
  Community* (2003) 67–9, 74–5,
  78
Amadiba Crisis Committee 12, 31
Amadiba Tribal Authority 31
apartheid 21, 24, 27, 33, 43–4,
  100, 102, 109, 112
arable land 50, 64, 90–1, 167
Atuahene, Bernadette 131

B

Bakgatla (chieftaincy) 11, 76–7, 79
Bakgatla Tribal Authority 76
Balepye-Maenetja (community)
  104, 107
Bam, Fikile 68, 70–1, 77, 129
Bantu Authorities 5
Bantu Authorities Act (1951) 18,
  98–9
BaPhalaborwa (community)
  105–7
Bapo-ba-Mogale 12
  mining agreements of 11
Bennett, Tom
  Customary Law in South Africa
  (2004) 16
Bill of Rights 79
Bizana 12, 46–7, 50, 68, 71,
  111–12
Black Communities Development
  Act (1984) 33–4
Black Economic Empowerment
  (BEE) 11, 31, 153
Bophuthatswana 35–6, 49
Bophuthatswana Bantustan 11–12
Border Rural Committee 111
Botshabelo
  upgrading of 36
Budlender, Debbie
  survey of rural land markets 46

Budlender, Geoff 17

C
Cape Colony 22
Cape Town 12
Capps, Gavin 11
chieftaincy 17–18, 29, 31, 43, 69, 84–5, 97–8, 106, 112, 128, 152
 inclusion in CPAs 41
 political frameworks focusing on 99, 111
Chiloane, Chief 105
Ciskei 22, 35–6, 38–9
Commission for the Restitution of Land Rights 110–11
Commission on the Communal Land Tenure Bill (2016) 152
Communal Land Rights Act (CLARA)(2004) 15, 24, 37, 67, 153–4
 criticisms of 37
Communal Land Rights Bill
 proposed provisions for 61–2
communal land tenure 13, 15, 17, 20, 31–2, 35, 50, 53, 61, 66–75, 80, 87–9, 129, 160–1, 164–5, 172
Communal Land Tenure Bill (2017) 3, 154, 158, 160, 162–3, 169–70
 Communal Land Boards 168–9
 Households Forum 168
 provisions of 160–1, 164–5, 167–8
communal property associations (CPAs) 24, 45, 61, 65–6, 72–5, 85, 95–6, 101, 118, 121–2, 124, 129–30, 136–7, 146–7, 151, 168–9
 Act (1996), 24, 136
 artificially-created 118
 committees 43
 dysfunctional 137, 142
 family landholdings in 25
 inclusion of chiefs in 41
 issues of upgrading 41
communities 4, 9, 100–2, 104, 106, 120
 benefit distribution 11
 peri-urban 9–10, 61, 148, 155
 rural 1, 9–10, 155
Constitution (1996) 1–3, 9, 15, 26, 39, 53, 67, 75–7, 79, 88, 99, 119, 160, 164, 167
Constitutional Court 37–40, 66, 71, 75–6, 79, 95, 98, 119, 126, 133, 144, 150–1
customary tenure 1, 10, 15, 24, 28, 56, 67, 70, 74, 84, 109, 157
 legislation 35, 68
 living 151–2

D
Deeds Office 2, 14, 23, 35, 37–9, 43, 53, 61, 155, 161, 166, 171
 proposed development of 58
Deeds Registry 21–2, 53, 57–8
Deeds Registry Act (1937) 35, 38
 provisions of 60
Department of Agriculture 90
Department of Co-operative Governance 52
Department of Justice 29
Department of Land Affairs 26,

INDEX

52, 110, 118
Department of Rural
  Development and Land
  Reform (DRDLR) 29, 41, 51,
  56, 58, 72, 122, 149, 161, 171
Dodson, Alan 68–9, 120

E
East London 36
Eastern Cape 10, 12–13, 16, 21–2,
  37, 47, 61, 64–5, 68, 72, 78, 111,
  121, 129–30, 152, 156, 163
Eastern Cape High Court 78
Extension of Security of Tenure
  Act 62 (ESTA)(1997) 27, 35

F
family landholdings 13, 25, 60,
  68, 75
  within CPAs 25
Fort Hare 65
Free State 36, 88–9

G
Gauteng 10, 81
Ghana 48, 153
Glen Grey Act (1894) 22, 61, 163
Group Areas Act 3, 109

H
Hanekom, Derek
  Minister for Land Affairs 110
*Hlolweni et al. vs North
  Pondoland Sugar* (2010) 68–72,
  74, 77–8, 129–30
homeland policy 98–9
household rights 16

Houses of Traditional Leaders
  99, 132
Hunter, Monica
  Reaction to Conquest (1936) 16

I
Imizizi (chieftancy) 69–70
individual/quitrent tenure 2, 22,
  40, 156, 163
  right to upgrade 38–9
informal landholdings/
  settlements 27
  protections for 35
  upgrading of 36–7
  use of PIE legislation 27
Ingonyama Trust
  23, 25, 28, 35, 153
Integrated Development Plan for
  Mopani District (2016) 88
Interim Protection of Informal
  Land Rights Act 31 (IPILRA)
  (1996) 26, 29–32, 35, 53, 55, 70,
  73, 75, 149, 155, 157, 170
  reinforcement of 72–3
  shortcomings of 28
International Federation of
  Surveyors 54

J
James, Deborah 44, 112
Jongilanga Tribal Authority 103,
  105

K
Kenya
  Machakos 50, 65
Kerr, A.J. 17, 98, 151

187

Khoi nation 134
King William's Town 22, 38
Kingwill, Rosalie 22–3, 149
Korana (ethnic group) 134
Krige, Eileen 16
KwaZulu-Natal 21, 23, 27–8, 49, 101, 110, 112, 114, 121–2, 163
KwaZulu-Natal Legislative Assembly
  Ingonyama Trust Act 3 (1994) 23, 25, 28, 35, 153

L

labour tenants 27, 120
Land Claims Commission (LCC) 3, 95, 110, 113–15, 117–18, 124, 131, 134, 143
  Regional (RLCC) 103, 110, 114
Land Claims Court 31, 68, 103, 110, 117, 119, 126, 144–6, 150
land ownership, 2, 15–20, 24–5, 31, 34–6, 38–40, 44, 51, 57, 59–60, 64, 67–75, 81, 83, 87, 89, 98, 101, 105, 126, 129, 145, 149, 150–1, 155–6, 158, 161–2, 164–5, 169–70
land markets, 36, 44–6, 48, 51, 58, 81, 85, 128, 166,
Land Records Act
  proposals for 53–8, 149, 158
land redistribution 1, 3, 5–6, 24, 66, 130
land restitution 1, 3–4, 17, 95, 99, 109, 112–13, 131, 138–9, 143–4
  legal case judgments 65–6, 68, 74
  reopening of 131–3
  settlements 139

Land Restitution Amendment Bill (2013) 133–4, 144
  public hearing (2013) 132
  validation of 144
land tenure 1–3, 14, 16–17, 66, 95, 97, 148, 158–61, 164
  communal tenure – *see* communal land tenure
  customary 16
  insecurity issues 53
  PTO 21–2
  role of spatial reorganisation in 64–5
Land Titles Adjustment Act (1993)
  proposed updating of 58
  provisions of 49
Legal Resources Centre 12, 17, 28, 68, 150
Limpopo 10, 16, 46, 64–5, 80, 85, 89, 103, 111, 113, 133, 136–8

M

Mabunda, David 126–7
Machoga vs Potgietersrus Platinum (2006)
  findings of 29–31
Majeje Tribal Authority 104
Makuba 133
Mala Mala 125–7
Malatji, Kgoshi Brown 133
Mandela, Nelson 52
Manona, Siyabu 28–9, 31–2, 149
Mdantsane 41–2
  upgrading of 36
Mgwali 40–1
  attempts at upgrading 40, 42

INDEX

Mhlanganisweni (community) 103, 105–6, 125–6
Mineral and Petroleum Resources Development Act 28 (2002) 10, 12
mining 31, 151–2
   platinum 11
Mlondobozi, Norah 87, 91
Mnisi Traditional Authority 103–5
Mnwana, Sonwabile 11
Moguerane, Khumisho 'A Home of Their Own' 45
Moletele (community) 103, 106–7
Mopani 82, 86
Mopani Farmers' Association (MFA) 87, 91
Motlanthe, Kgalema 135
Mozambique 133
Mpondo (ethnic group) 16, 69
Mpondoland 98–9
Mpumalanga 13, 27, 133
Mthatha 22

N

Natal 2
National Land Ombud
   proposals for 54
National Parks Board 126
National Party 33
National Planning Committee 22
Native Trust and Land Act (1936) 18–19, 63
Natives Land Act (1913) 3, 33, 95, 114, 134
   abolition of (1991) 3
Nkwinti, Gugile 5

Minister for Rural Development and Land Reform 4
North West Province 10
Ntuli, Philile 23
Nkuzi Development Association 111, 116

O

off-register tenure 26–7, 31–2, 52, 54, 160
   categories of black landholders 34
   peri-urban 150
   proposed rights for 55
   rural 150
   variants of 24–5
ownership – *see* land ownership

P

Parliament 9, 132–3, 135, 140, 146
Permission to Occupy (PTO) 10, 19–21, 25, 27–8, 32, 35, 45–7, 66, 81, 83–4, 87, 89, 109, 150, 157, 163
   land allocations made by 19–20, 40
   land tenure 21–2
   shortcomings of 20–1
   view as 'deed of grant' 83
Phetole, Mamatlepa 139
Pilane, Chief 11, 76
Pilane and Another vs Pilane and Another (2013) 77
poverty 46–7, 56, 112
Prevention of Illegal Eviction Act

19 (PIE)(1998) 27, 35, 55, 149
private property 46, 172
   costs of 48–9
   market 81
privatisation
   of rural land 47–8

R
Reconstruction and Development Programme (RDP) 24
   housing grants 171
   housing stock 34–7, 44, 48–9, 81–2, 158
   informal sale of houses 53
   titles for housing stock 57, 60
Regulatory Impact Assessment 122
rental market 85–6
Restitution of Land Rights Act (1994) 3–4, 31, 67–8, 72, 77, 83, 95ff
Restitution of Land Rights Amendment Act (2014) 3–4, 95, 99, 122, 158
   provisions of 119
Rustenburg 11

S
Sabi Sand Game Reserve 103, 107, 125
Setlhare (tribe) 105
settlement layouts 63
Sigcau, Botha 70
Sigwela, Ezra 111
smallholdings 14
Smith, Henk 68

Sotho (ethnic group) 105, 108
South Africa 15, 17, 26–7, 44–5, 50, 67–8, 70–1, 97, 148–9, 154–5
Soweto 33–4, 81
Spar
   Spar Rural Hub 91
spatial reorganisation 63
   role in tenure reform 64–5
Spatial Planning and Land Use Management Act 16 (SPLUMA)(2013) 55, 155

T
tenure security 9, 47, 53, 66, 80, 88, 90–1, 95, 153, 157
   role of political authority in 85
Thaba Nchu 41–2
   upgrading of 36
Thabina Irrigation Scheme 86
titling 43, 55, 165
   criticisms of 47–50, 59
   full 155
   private 43
traditional leaders 4, 78–9, 82, 85, 95, 98–9, 103, 111–2, 117–9, 129–32, 141–2, 152, 161–3, 168–70
Traditional Leadership and Governance Act, Eastern Cape (2005) 78
Traditional Leadership and Governance Framework Act (2003) 99, 163
Transkei 20, 22, 28, 35, 50, 68–9, 83, 112, 129
Transkei Development

INDEX

Corporation 129
Transkei Land Service Organisation (TRALSO) 111
Transvaal 18
Trengrove, Wim 68
trusts 10, 24–5, 41, 118, 122–4, 146
Tsonga (ethnic group) 105, 108, 133–4
Tswana (ethnic group) 16

U

Umhlaba Rural Services 36
undivided co-ownership 59
United Democratic Front (UDF) 109
University of Cape Town African Studies Centre 78
University of Witwatersrand Society, Work and Development Institute (SWOP) 10–11
Upgrading of Land Tenure Rights Act (ULTRA)(1991) 35–6, 42, 49, 155, 164, 166, 170
  amendment of (1996) 34
  amendment of (1998) 34, 166
  lack of implementation in rural areas 37–8

urban landholdings 45, 118
  Apartheid prohibitions of 44–5

V

VaMakhuva (community) 104–6
Venda 35

W

Walker, Cherryl 114–15
  Land Claims Commissioner for KwaZulu-Natal 101, 110
Wegerif, Mark 111
Western Cape 10, 134
Wild Coast Sun 69, 73, 122
Witwatersrand 10
women's land rights 13, 17, 45–6, 50, 60, 76, 80–1, 85, 88–91
  as co-owners 156
  as widows 21
  discrimination 15
  property purchases 88–9
  quitrent sites 39
Wotshela, Luvuyo 40

Z

Zion Christian Church 89
Zuma, Jacob 4, 99, 131–2
ZZ2 139–40